POLAR
ATTACK

POLAR ATTACK

From Canada to the North Pole, and Back

Richard Weber

and

Mikhail Malakhov

M&S

Canadian Cataloguing in Publication Data

Weber, Richard, 1959–
      Polar attack: from Canada to the North Pole, and back

ISBN 0-7710-8902-3

1. Weber, Richard, 1959–   . 2. Malakhov, Mikhail, 1955–   . 3. Arctic regions – Discovery and exploration – Canadian. 4. Arctic regions – Discovery and exploration – Russian. 5. North Pole. I. Malakhov, Mikhail, 1955-   . II. Title.

G630.C3W4 1996   910'.9163'2   C96-931174-5

The publishers acknowledge the support of the Canada Council and the Ontario Arts Council for their publishing program.

Map by the Geological Survey of Canada

Typesetting by M&S, Toronto
Printed and bound in Canada

McClelland & Stewart Inc.
The Canadian Publishers
481 University Avenue
Toronto, Ontario
M5G 2E9

1 2 3 4 5   00 99 98 97 96

To our sons, Misha and Aloysha, Tessum and Nansen,
in the hope that they will understand our journey

CONTENTS

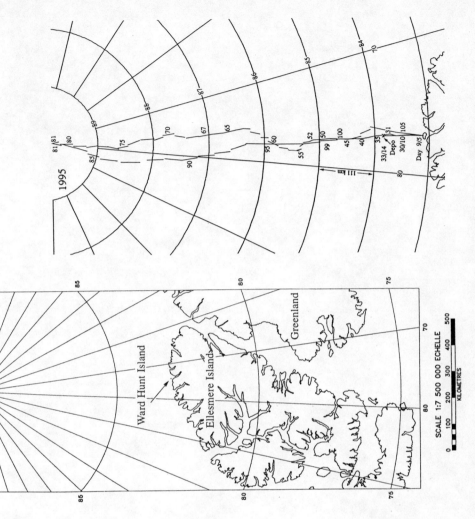

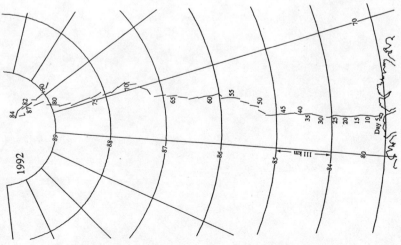

Note: The routes taken in 1992 and 1995 are indicated by broken lines, with the number of expedition days noted. The breaks indicate the amount of overnight drift.

PART
ONE

CHAPTER ONE

Once you get there, there's nothing to be seen — no flags, markers, or memorials, no trace of those who preceded you. Even if they left behind some evidence of their arrival, it's long gone, borne away by the ever-shifting ice. All around you stretches only measureless desolation. The silence is absolute; the only sounds are those you make, punctuated by the wind.

The North Pole looks exactly like a million other points on the Arctic Ocean. There's no particular grandeur to it, like a mountain peak. As the northern axis of the earth's rotation, it is a place that exists more in principle than in fact — a mere dot on the map, a purely mathematical concept. We have known that it is there since the time of the earliest astronomers, who pondered the heavens while sitting amid the olive groves. It wasn't until many hundreds of years later that anyone felt compelled to pay a visit. The sun circles continuously above the horizon for six months at a time, then disappears for six months more, which is spectacular enough — but much the same effect can be observed in greater comfort and safety farther south. All the world's time zones and all its lines of longitude converge there, at precisely 90°N. There is no direction but south. Greenland, the nearest patch of solid ground, is 400 miles (740 km) away.[*]

---

[*] All distances travelled on the Arctic Ocean are expressed in nautical miles. One nautical mile equals 1.15 statute miles, approximately 1.85 kilometres. A nautical mile also equals exactly one minute of latitude. There are sixty minutes in a degree of latitude; thus, the distance from eighty degrees to the Pole (at ninety degrees) is 600 miles (1,110 km). For convenience, latitudes (and longitudes, when they arise) are expressed in the text as follows: eighty-two degrees, fifteen minutes appears as 82°15'. Fractions of minutes have been rounded off, except in Appendix C.

There seems to be little point in bending superhuman efforts to arrive at so inhospitable a place. But men and women have been attempting to come here for centuries. They travelled by ship, by dogsled and balloon, by snowmobile and submarine. Some died; others were maimed and broken. At first they sought the North-west Passage to the Orient. When this hope proved illusory, they came for monarch and country, for personal glory, or in search of a polar grail. In 1896, an American named Walter Wellman, who abandoned journalism for Arctic exploration, wrote, "The quest for the North Pole is the all-compelling instinct to know all of the unknown, it matters not where. To make this unknown known is one of the highest ambitions of man." On the other

---

The distance from our departure point on Ward Hunt Island to the Pole is 415 nautical miles (768 km), including three miles (6 km) from shore to the point where the island's permanent ice shelf meets the pack ice. A complete round-trip therefore totals 830 miles (1,536 km). But this figure is extremely deceptive. In his book *Icewalk*, Robert Swan stated that he and his companions had to surmount at least 2,000 pressure ridges – steep and often jagged mounds of upthrust ice averaging five metres (16 ft.) in height. Thus, Swan's team travelled an additional ten kilometres (6 mi.) up and down. Any polar explorer spends a great deal of time climbing small mountains, and these "vertical distances" should be factored into the total.

As well, it's impossible for an expedition to progress in anything resembling a straight line. One must constantly detour in order to skirt expanses of open water or merely to scout out and follow a more promising path. Swan cited a study conducted by the well-known Arctic traveller Wally Herbert, who analysed Commander Robert Peary's expeditions and concluded that their "sideways" movements added 25 per cent to the distance covered en route. We take a slightly more conservative view, but probably covered an extra 20 per cent.

Also bear in mind that our expeditions were not confined to a series of forward or one-way marches. As we'll explain, we often went ahead with a partial load, left it by the trail, returned the way we'd come, and brought up the rest of our supplies. This back-and-forth shuttle added hugely to the total distance. We estimate that we covered 1,200 miles (2,220 km) during our second, successful expedition, but we can't be sure. A pedometer isn't effective if you're both walking and skiing, and any sort of device attached to a sled would have broken down. In other words, you'll have to take our word for it.

hand, a lot of people set off for the Pole quite simply because, like Everest, it happened to be there.

In 1988, we had stood at the Pole together for the first time, as members of the thirteen-man Soviet–Canadian expedition known as Polar Bridge, which was the first successful journey, on foot and on skis, across the top of the world from northern Siberia to Ellesmere Island National Park Reserve. During the course of this journey, we became close friends, despite the difference in our backgrounds and ages – Richard was then twenty-eight, and Misha, thirty-three. But we were drawn to each other immediately, in part because Misha was by far the most outgoing and worldly member of the Soviet team, eager to make contact with his western counterparts and to learn about and experiment with unfamiliar equipment and techniques rather than rely on traditional (and in some cases outmoded) methods. Each of us recognized the other's strengths as a polar traveller. In 1986, Richard had been a member of Will Steger's landmark expedition, which went one-way from Canada by ski and dogsled. He and his teammate, Brent Boddy, were the first Canadians to reach the top of the world on foot. Misha, who'd trained as a thoracic surgeon, had served as a physician at a Soviet Antarctic research facility. In 1986, he'd skied with the Soviet Polar Night expedition, sponsored by *Komsomolskaya Pravda*, the Communist youth newspaper. This group journeyed about 400 miles (740 km) in total darkness during January and February, groping their way along by means of handheld flashlights. But our real bond in 1988 was the fact that we wanted to learn each other's language.

One day, before we'd actually reached the Pole, Misha was pondering his well-thumbed Russian–English dictionary when Richard paused in his attempts to fathom the Cyrillic alphabet and began to muse aloud. "You know," he said, "the ice on this side seems fairly easy to deal with. It's not nearly as rough as over by the Canadian coast. I wonder if it's possible to reach the Pole on foot without the help of aircraft."

Misha was unimpressed; the idea seemed to him far-fetched in the extreme. Aircraft were absolutely indispensable, our lifeline to the outside world. Steger's expedition had been unsupplied, it's true – but its three tonnes of food and equipment were hitched up to almost fifty dogs. Every other modern polar expedition had been supplied by air. Every two weeks during Polar Bridge, a plane would land beside us on the ice, or, if it was not equipped to land on the ice or it couldn't for lack of a suitable landing strip – for example, if we were in the middle of rough or unstable ice, or surrounded by open water – then foodstuffs, fuel, and replacement items could still be parachuted down or simply thrown from the plane as it made a low-altitude pass. The thought of carrying with us everything necessary to get to the Pole seemed quite absurd. If you were going to try it, you needed dogs – that was the rule, the accepted wisdom. An unsupported journey on foot and on skis was out of the question. No one had ever done it – except for a hopeless attempt by Sir Ranulph Fiennes in 1986 – and it was probably madness to try.

In any case, we had no time to dwell on implausible schemes. Our minds were fixed on the immediate goal, which was itself highly unusual. Early adventurers, of course, had been forced to make their way back to where they started from, but late-twentieth-century explorers, no matter how they travelled, had been airlifted out when the journey was over. On the one hand, this made perfect sense. You reached (or quite often didn't reach) the Pole. That was your goal; having achieved it, or taken your best shot, it was time to go home. On the other hand, though, the idea seemed truncated – a halfway measure with no parallel elsewhere. Mountain climbers, for example, aren't whisked away by helicopter when they reach the top. Rather, they have to clamber down the way they came. Polar Bridge would be the exception to this rule — like the battery-powered pink rabbit, we just kept on going. As Richard had observed, conditions were somewhat easier on the Russian side, even though the distance from land to Pole is appreciably greater than it is from Canada. The "Russian" ice is flatter, younger, thinner, and less daunting. In places it's almost boring; you just put your head down and plod along. As well, the drift on the Russian side tends to take you where you want to go — northward, towards the Pole. You don't wake up in the morning and find that you've been driven back four miles (7 km) overnight, as is the case on the Canadian side, where a southeast drift prevails. Of course, within the context of Polar Bridge, this meant only that the second half of the expedition would be the more arduous — but once we'd crossed over the Pole and were heading for Canada, we were, in effect, making a return trip, and Richard began to muse on this notion as well.

Nor would the idea of an unsupported expedition go away. As the Polar Bridge team moved south, Christopher Holloway, another Canadian member, said that an Australian named Dick Smith was rumoured to have offered $500,000 to anybody who managed to reach the Pole on foot without outside assistance. But rumours are nothing to pin your hopes on, and the matter was pushed to the back of our minds until Polar Bridge was over.

The following year, 1989, Misha was back in the Arctic again as a member of Icewalk — an eight-man international expedition organized by our friend Robert Swan, who hoped to become the first person to reach both poles on foot and to alert the public to the dangers of environmental depredation that threatened even the most remote regions of the planet. Icewalk — a one-way march from the Canadian side — was supplied by air as well. During it, Misha made an interesting discovery. For the first time, he managed to travel in something approaching comfort, with a relative lack of suffering. Because of Icewalk's environmental mandate, the tasks to be performed en route were even more numerous and complicated than those that had occupied him during Polar Bridge, but he found himself deriving real pleasure from the knowledge that the planning and equipment were as good as they could be, so we could avoid all unnecessary suffering – a major step forward from the psychological point of view. Nonetheless, he could not entirely dispel a feeling that (in the words of a Russian proverb) he was "entering the same river twice." He feared from time to time that he was repeating himself; that he had "been there, done that" – an odd thing to say about an adventure of such magnitude. When Icewalk ended, Misha at first believed that he wouldn't travel to the Pole again – until he turned to the pages of Robert Peary's diary. "The process of reaching the North Pole," Peary wrote, "may be identified with a game of chess, where all the moves, leading to a favourable outcome, have been thoroughly thought out in advance, long before the beginning of the game." Reading these words, Misha understood immediately that, just as any chess game is subject to an almost infinite number of variables, no two polar journeys could be alike in every respect, even though their routes were virtually identical and the details more or less the same. Each expedition brings fresh challenge and new insight. No wonder, then, that yet another variable – the idea that an expedition could go (or even go and come back) relying entirely on its own resources – began to assume a measure of plausibility in his mind.

Meanwhile, Richard had not been idle. While Misha was busy with Icewalk, Richard was drifting happily overhead as part of an expedition organized by the environmental group Global Concern, led by Paul Lavelle. The team members flew to within twenty miles (37 km) of the Pole, skied in the rest of the way, and launched a hot-air balloon that bore the message: "Save the Ozone – Use Ozone-Safe." History was repeating itself. In 1896 and 1897, a Swede named Salomon Andrée had tried his luck in a helium-filled balloon made of Chinese silk. He crashed during his second flight and tried to walk to safety, but died en route – apparently because he killed a polar bear and ate its liver. (A useful tip: polar bear liver is toxic to humans.)

During the Global Concern trip, Richard had found himself in Resolute Bay, where he'd bumped into Dick Smith, the allegedly philanthropic Australian. Smith was the publisher of *Australian Geographic* magazine, had helped fund several previous expeditions (including Swan's to Antarctica), and happened to be in Resolute Bay because he himself was flying around the world, Pole to Pole, in a Twin Otter – that seemingly ageless workhorse of northern aviation. Smith clarified the rumours of a cash prize, but attached a number of very important strings.

"Normally, I help Australians do things in Australia," he said. "I won't help you in this way; there'll be no money up front. You tell me you might try to go to the Pole unsupported. That's fine, and I don't care how you do it; you can use skidoos, skis, or dogs – anything you pick. If you use dogs, you can't kill them, that's the first rule. The second rule is – I'm not interested in a one-way trip. You've done it already, with Will Steger. But if you get to the Pole and back, like Peary, it would be worth $200,000."

Well, there we were. But where exactly were we? In the first place, we had very little desire to emulate Peary. His expedition resembled a military invasion. Advance parties went ahead of him carrying equipment and food, marked out a trail, and constructed igloos and way stations along his path. He treated the Arctic as his private fiefdom, abused the Inuit, refused to recognize the contribution of his companion, Matthew Henson, and butchered many of his 133 dogs as he went, feeding the weaker animals to the stronger ones (hence Smith's proviso). Despite these grandiose procedures, Peary almost certainly didn't reach the Pole at all (see Appendix D). But that wasn't the point. He may not have got there, but there's no denying that he came back. Smith's major ground rule was plain: Not only would we have to attain the Pole, taking with us every gram of food and drop of fuel, we'd have to return under our own steam. Fair enough. The fact was, no one had done it. The question was, could it be done? We decided to try.

Others were thinking about it, too, and the clock was running. In 1989, Ranulph Fiennes had made his third attempt to reach the Pole one-way without outside support. Fiennes is a world-renowned traveller and adventurer, with extensive experience in the Antarctic. Between 1979 and 1982, like some character out of a Jules Verne novel, he had circled the globe north to south, along the Greenwich Meridian, by every means possible — Jeeps, ships, rubber rafts, snowmobiles, and everything short of camels. He had been knighted for this and other exploits; his proper title is Sir Ranulph. But he'd failed utterly to master the Arctic ice. Asked to compare the two poles, Fiennes had replied that there wasn't any comparison. "It is doubtless much colder in the extreme south," he said, "but there you are sure to feel solid ground beneath your feet." He was, of course, correct: Antarctica is a continent, not an ocean. It's basically one great big ice cap; once you get up the mountains that ring the perimeter, it's plain sailing — one of the reasons why most South Pole expeditions succeed their first time around. In the Arctic, the reverse is true.

Fiennes's sense of unease was echoed and amplified by Robert Swan, whose private diaries from Icewalk record his struggles with the polar sea: "Sometimes amidst all this ice rubble and black spots of open water it would seem to me impossible for a human being to survive. And so I feel like lying down and dying. It is much more difficult here than in the Antarctic." Swan's great courage and sense of purpose are recognized by everyone who knows him, and his words offer eloquent testimony to the perils that lay ahead of us, should we choose to accept the challenge.

If we didn't, someone else would. The Pole was becoming a destination of choice. In 1968-69, Wally Herbert had successfully travelled across it en route from Alaska to Spitsbergen, Norway. He and his companions had wintered on the ice, travelling by ski and dogsled. Also in 1968, Ralph Plaisted went one-way by snowmobile. A Russian team headed by Dmitri Shparo made it one-way on skis in 1979, the same year that Niomi Umura made a fifty-five-day solo return trip with dogs. Ann Bancroft marched with the Steger expedition, becoming the first woman to reach the Pole itself. In 1986, an all-female expedition attempted to set off from Spitsbergen. Unsuccessful, they were airlifted some distance onto the ice. They battled the current for weeks, but were swept back past their starting point, thus putting an end to approaches from that direction. Also in 1986, Jean-Louis Étienne made the first successful solo march hauling his own sled, but he was supported by airdrops all the way. In 1990, a trio of Norwegians almost went unsupported on foot one-way, but one of them was injured and had to be evacuated. These guys were our major worry; were they to try it again, they'd be a force to be reckoned with.

As would the Arctic itself. The Arctic Ocean isn't frozen solid. This comes as a rude surprise to many people, who quite reasonably assume that, since it's so damn cold up there, the surface must surely be locked into immobility. Nothing could be further from the truth.

From the air, the ocean invites a host of similes. It looks like a jigsaw puzzle, a patchwork quilt, a maze. The white surface is crazed with thousands of dark lines. These lines are open water.

Far from being one solid mass, all 5 million square miles (13 mil. km²) of ocean are composed of an infinite number of individual pieces of ice. These can be enormous or very small. Floes are smaller, pans are larger, but everything regardless of size is in more or less perpetual motion, under the influence of tides, currents, the moon, and prevailing winds. Three-metre-thick (10-ft.-thick) ice throbs and vibrates uncannily beneath your feet.

The open water goes by various names. Cracks are relatively narrow; half the time, you simply hop across them. A "lead" is a big crack. It can be as wide as a city street or a multilane highway. Sometimes you can't see the other side. Your salvation lies in the fact that leads tend to be wide, not long. They've got a beginning and an end; you can walk around them sometimes in a few minutes, occasionally in a few hours. The worst barriers are persistent cracks that go on forever. But leads can open and close with lightning speed, their edges forced apart or squeezed together by movement in the waters below. When they're squeezed together, the effect is like an earthquake at sea or, more accurately, like the movement of tectonic plates on land. That's how mountains were created, back in the mists of time. On the ocean, when ice meets ice, the edges are thrust up into pressure ridges the height of two- or three-storey buildings. If you're on the scene, you can watch it happen before your very eyes. Then you try to find a way around them. Most of the time, there is no "around," and you have to scale the ramparts, or find a pathway through, along the floor of an ice canyon with sheer walls to either side. It's hard to describe in everyday words what the Arctic is about. For example, the rather innocuous phrase "ice rubble" translates as something that looks like the aftermath of saturation bombing – vast plains of frozen boulders big as compact cars.

All these exertions take place amid temperatures of $-50°C$ ($-58°F$), with windchills that approach $-120°C$ ($-184°F$). Exposed flesh freezes in seconds. Navigation and communication equipment, which is battery-powered, is slow to respond. Bear that in mind the next time your car won't start on a mildly frosty morning.

Above a latitude of 85°, the Arctic is by definition a semi-desert. It receives on average between ten and twenty centimetres

(4 and 8 in.) of precipitation annually. Some years are less average than others. Whatever falls doesn't melt. It stays in place, forming waist-deep drifts or small, undulating patterns called sastrugi, which look harmless enough, unless you happen to be dragging a heavily loaded sled.

Sometimes the surface of a lead will freeze, and you can ski along it – a nice, smooth pathway like fresh pavement. Sometimes it won't, and you cross the water by rolling in blocks of ice, then filling the gaps with snow to form a makeshift bridge. Sometimes you can hopscotch across on floating "stepping-stones" or choose one to serve as a raft. Sometimes you ski, not on ice or snow, but on slush – an insidious surface that's been temporarily pressed together and will bear your weight as long as you stay in motion or until whatever is exerting the pressure decides to stop. If you hesitate or hit a weakened patch (which you can't see, because of the fog, blizzard, or white-out haze), you may fall through. If so, there's nothing for you to grab on to and heave yourself out to safety; you'll flounder in frigid quicksand with nothing beneath it but a watery grave.

Welcome, as Robert Swan so eloquently put it, to a place that wants you dead.

But all of this was old hat to us. We knew the risks, and we were prepared to up the ante – to make things ever harder on ourselves. In 1989, we began to consider seriously the logistics of a round-trip unsupported expedition.

In the first place, how would we travel? We did not wish to go by snowmobile, which would involve towing vast quantities of fuel. Neither of us had had much to do with dogs, barring Richard's experiences with Steger. Skis were the preferred method of transport. Both of us were experts – Richard had been skiing since he was two years old, had joined the Canadian National

Cross-Country Ski Team in 1977, and had retired with twenty national titles to his credit after representing Canada in four world championships. Nothing could be more ecologically responsible; you exploit no one but yourself. So that much, at least, was settled at the outset.

Next we had to ask: If a return trip were possible, where should we go from and come back to? As we've said, the ice on the Russian side is smoother, more easily dealt with. But a return trip from Russia wasn't practical – because Cape Arkticheskiy, the northernmost point in Siberia, is too far south. It lies below the line of permanent pack ice, and we wouldn't be able to get back to land after early April because our way would be blocked by open water. (Once, Steger tried to leave in mid-March; the ice was already breaking up.) To avoid this, we'd have to start off during the Boxing Day sales.

As well, the Russian side of things wasn't what you might call rich in history. The area wasn't even discovered until just before the First World War. No expeditions left from there until the 1930s. A Canadian route posed by far the greater challenge, but that's the way that Peary and all the rest of the early adventurers had come. So had most of our immediate predecessors. The jumping-off point was either Cape Columbia, on the tip of Elles-mere Island, or Ward Hunt, a tiny island lying just off Ellesmere at 83°05', thus making it the northernmost point of land in Canada. Cape Columbia had a landing strip, but nothing else (other than Peary's signpost, which points the way to various major cities worldwide, and an ammunition box in which depart-ing expeditions have traditionally placed their farewell messages). At least Ward Hunt – a former military and meteorological base – had two crude huts in which other explorers, most recently Fiennes, had taken temporary shelter. So we circled Ward Hunt on an Arctic map and congratulated ourselves on our progress.

All throughout 1990 and into 1991, we conferred in person and by telephone and E-mail. (Misha was one of the first Russians to set up an E-mail link, back in the days when few people anywhere knew what it was or exactly how it worked.) A thousand details were thrashed out at a distance. Imagine two people on opposite sides of the globe trying to plan an unprecedented adventure of extreme complexity while striving to earn their respective livings. Misha had numerous business as well as medical interests (as did his wife, Olga, an ophthalmologist); Richard and his wife, Josée, were busy with a small company called Polar Challenge, which modified, designed, and manufactured outdoor equipment. Real life intruded, and the prospective start date began to be postponed over and over again.

To begin with, we set out to determine exactly how many supplies would be needed to sustain us for an expedition totalling 100 days, start to finish. No manna would descend from heaven at two-week intervals; we would have to take with us everything we needed. The list was exhaustive – food and fuel, stoves, cooking utensils, a tent, sleeping bags and pads, clothing, navigation and communication devices, and so forever on. How much would all this weigh? How much weight could conceivably be carried (or, more accurately, carried in backpacks and towed on sleds) by two humans through the worst that the Arctic could throw at us? (This was, after all, our bright idea, and we began by assuming that there'd only be the two of us. By the way, neither of us wanted to make a solo attempt; it demands a very special frame of mind.) We crunched the numbers as best we could and came up with a gross weight in excess of 300 kilograms (661 lb.). Each of us would have to bear in one way or another half that total – in other words, more than twice our body weight.

What else could we do? There was no way to shave the total by an appreciable amount; all these things were absolutely necessary. Our supplies would fill two backpacks and four sleds to overflowing. We knew that we wouldn't be capable of carrying them all at once through the roughest patches – but we could resort to shuttle trips during at least the initial stages of the journey, taking part of the load forward, leaving it beside the trail, and returning for the rest. As we moved along, the weight would lessen daily as we consumed our food and fuel rations. Eventually, we'd be able to repack the remainder into one sled and backpack each. So far, so good; but the more we thought about it, the more we began to consider seriously the advantages of spreading the weight around by enlarging the expedition to include a number of participants.

Say, for example, that the common load – everything other than personal foods – totalled forty kilograms (88 lb.) per man. If a third person were along for the march, we'd all carry proportionately less. If a fourth could be recruited, the figure became a mere ten kilograms (22 lb.). And if a fifth or sixth team member could be persuaded to join us . . . but here we stopped. It would be hard enough to find two other people whose experience and proven skills would enable them to survive. But a four-man team sounded more or less right, and this became our target.

We made a list and began to discuss potential candidates. We knew all too well that the Arctic Ocean is a place apart, as Swan and Fiennes had confirmed. Nothing can prepare you for it; success elsewhere, even in Antarctica, doesn't transpose. (Nor does any other form of physical prowess. If either of us set out to climb Everest or K-2, we would almost certainly die.) We're talking about a club with very limited membership: not all that many people have been up there and come back in one piece. We thought first of our companions from previous trips, but most of them were busy paying off the mortgage, planning explorations of their own, or convinced that they wouldn't go back even with a gun held to their heads – let alone as part of someone else's unsupported expedition. Frankly, many people thought that we were tilting at Arctic windmills. Will Steger said flatly that it couldn't be done — a view he repeated to the board of *National Geographic* magazine, with the result that it didn't follow our efforts. Steger has since changed his mind, but it's a pity that neither of our expeditions got the coverage we thought they deserved.

If you spend a month on the ice with a man, you come to know him better than you would during years in an urban environment. Every good quality will emerge at once; every shortcoming will be apparent as well. We had the greatest confidence in each other — but the introduction of third and fourth parties was fraught with pitfalls. As the months passed, the shortlist of prospective team members got very short indeed. Eventually, though, we managed to settle on our third man — Bob Mantell. He was a thirty-eight-year-old American, an enthusiastic dogsledder and Outward Bound instructor who lived in northern Minnesota. He had set off for the Pole with Richard in 1986, as part of Steger's expedition, and had plenty of prior experience in the North, both with other groups and on his own. His physical endurance was not in question — although in 1986 he'd suffered severe frostbite to his feet and had been airlifted out before he could reach the Pole. But Richard believed that he would make a valuable contribution to the team, and Bob accepted our belated invitation with the utmost eagerness.

The next and final person to join was John Mordhorst, aged forty-four. Although also an American, he was then the program director of Outward Bound Western Canada. He had spent an entire year travelling through the Arctic, overwintering in the barrens with two companions. While he was quietly sitting on the banks of the Thelon River, the debris from a malfunctioning Soviet satellite fell almost directly on top of him. He was swarmed by Canadian and American military personnel, flown to an Edmonton laboratory, debriefed, subjected to every test known to science, and then returned to the point from which he'd been evacuated. He felt (with some cause) that if he could survive these troubles, the Pole would hold no terrors for him – although he had not been there with any previous expedition.

In 1991, while Misha minded the store at home in Ryazan, a city about 200 kilometres (124 mi.) southeast of Moscow, Richard began to hold training sessions with Bob and John, both near his home outside Ottawa and later on Baffin Island, where they skied 600 kilometres (373 mi.) from Igloolik to Clyde River. At one point, Misha passed through Ottawa and nodded approvingly, but that was the extent of his involvement in the pre-expedition phase. Richard's diary recorded the group's progress and illustrates his optimism: "Bob is now stronger in physical and morale aspects than during the Steger expedition. He is aware of his capabilities and governs his body well. He is a very good skier. One day I was astonished to see that he was walking beside me at the same pace that I was skiing. He is less reserved than before, and becomes more sociable every day. He is meticulous, which will help him in his task as navigator. . . . John copes well with the radio link. He adapts himself well to varied situations. He is strong and his spirits are high; he makes himself useful at all times. He has insufficient experience in the Arctic, and must become more confident on skis. But by the time we leave, he will be in better shape, and the problems he experiences now should lessen over time."

But time was passing, and we held a press conference that announced our plans to the world. When the media grasped what we were setting out to do, they asked whether we were patterning ourselves on the classic expeditions of the past. Peary's name kept coming up, and we felt almost like spoilsports; we had to break the bad news that he wasn't necessarily the conqueror of the Pole. Certainly the idea of man-hauling our supplies suggested a throwback to simpler days. Circa the quest for a northwest passage, an expedition led by Sir William Parry (not to be confused with Peary, although everybody does) went sailing off in full-dress uniform, travelling across the ice by means of "sledge boats" — enormous contraptions that looked like Noah's Ark. Each one weighed in at 658 kilograms (1,450 lb.) and was six metres long by two metres wide (20 ft. × 7 ft.), mounted on iron-shod runners. After an unsuccessful experiment involving reindeer, the sledges were pulled — heaven knows how — by teams of a dozen seamen, who struggled in harness like so many oxen. No wonder his expedition turned back at around 82°45' — about 400 miles (740 km) from the Pole. We explained that, while we were in awe of these journeys, we would be unwise to re-enact them in every particular, like people who go out on the weekends and stage Civil War battles. To do so would have been manifestly absurd. For Robert Peary, Roald Amundsen, and Fridtjof Nansen, it was a tremendous feat merely to reach the jumping-off point of choice. We would be on the shores of Ward Hunt in a matter of hours. Our flights were the very least of our worries — merely a series of entries (and worrying enough, come to that) on our financial plan, of which more in a moment.

Nor could our equipment possibly be compared with that of the Arctic pioneers. For example, our sleds (unlike Sir Parry's behemoths) were slightly shorter and deeper than a cartop luggage carrier, but much the same idea. In fact, they were a slightly thicker version of a kid's sled marketed under the brand name Norcaboggan, which could be bought for ten dollars apiece at the nearest Canadian Tire store. Each was actually two sleds sandwiched together, top to bottom. This made a nice, rigid unit, which, while it wouldn't float, would survive a minor ducking.

But, in another sense, our expedition did indeed recall the experiences of our predecessors. It would be a supreme test of will — a triumph (or so we hoped and believed) of the human spirit in the face of tremendous odds. What did we seek to gain; what would we derive from our attempt? Nansen wrote that a person seeking "peace, eternity and freedom" would discover it "only in the high latitudes of the earth." That might be so — but only at the cost of constant, almost unimaginable exertions. Peary, continuing with his favourite metaphor, wrote that, in a chess game, one player's mental powers are pitted against the other's, whereas in the search for the Pole, "the struggle takes place between brain and will, and the blind rough forces of the primitive elements." We knew that our journey would test the limits of our physical and mental reserves. We ourselves were the *terra incognita*.

When Richard had stood at the Pole during Polar Bridge, he'd spoken on behalf of the entire Canadian team: "What draws us to this unique point? The Pole holds a powerful secret that has fascinated mankind since its existence was first revealed. The secret is different for all who rediscover it. To earn its familiarity requires time, unswerving motivation, and considerable hardship. We have not conquered the Pole; indeed, any surrender or any adaptation that has taken place has been within us." Could we withstand fresh hardships and not retreat? That and a thousand other questions would be answered only when we set foot on the ocean of ice.

CHAPTER TWO

Only someone who has actually travelled to the Arctic can hope to grasp its fascination. But, having touched its cold mystery, that person knows that no one would seek material benefits in the realm of ice. Unfortunately, back in the outside world, the bills fall due, and polar expeditions cost enormous sums of money.

We had a four-man team, ready to risk everything in pursuit of an elusive goal. We had the will to accomplish that end. We didn't have $200,000 (Can.) – our best estimate of what the expedition would cost. (This was the bargain of the year: Will Steger's expedition was budgeted at $600,000, and Icewalk – admittedly a much larger and more complex operation – came in at $7 million.)

For example, a single ticket from Toronto to Iqaluit cost $1,000 – actually, rather more when the airline got through with our excess baggage. A flight from Iqaluit to Resolute Bay was an additional $1,000. The next and final air link to Ward Hunt Island was $15,000. We multiplied all these sums times four and stared at them with ever-increasing dismay.

Next we had to hire a support staff. If you're going to be away for a while at the Pole, you'd better have a fully equipped office space, an expedition manager who'll oversee a multitude of details, and at least one radio operator located somewhere in the outside world. The bills begin mounting well in advance of your departure date; think of the telephone calls and fax transmissions alone. We kept our costs absurdly low, thanks partly to our friends and families who volunteered their time and energies – but over a period of many months, the pennies added up to startling sums.

Some of our equipment was donated by generous manufacturers who rightly expected to derive some publicity value if we succeeded in our attempt. These firms are duly thanked in Appendix G. We had to spend several thousand dollars on foodstuffs, but not as much as we'd initially feared. We greatly appreciated every donation to our fund in cash or kind, no matter how great or modest. Each was an eloquent demonstration of faith that we would succeed – and proved again and again that the expedition wasn't only our personal crusade but a matter of some. importance to others as well. This thought would sustain us in many a dark moment. We owed these people more than we could repay, and we kept on going in part because if we weakened and failed in the test, we felt that we'd be failing them, too.

One of our earliest sponsors was Kaufman Footwear, the well-known maker of quality winter boots. We met with Jack Thomas, vice-president of sales and marketing, who said that he liked the looks of the project but expected that we'd wear his products: boots sold under the brand name Sorel. Richard replied that they were fine boots for most occasions, but were less than ideal out on the polar ice. To his credit, Thomas not only took this criticism in stride but saw a way to turn it to his firm's advantage. He introduced Richard to Jim Chadwick, Kaufman's designer. Together they devised a new boot – the Weber– Malakhov Mukluk – that's proved, thanks to advanced technology, a "breathable" nylon surface, and all-synthetic "breathable" insulating liners instead of wool felt, to be the warmest cold-weather footwear in the world. It was subjected to extensive tests under horrible conditions during our early training sessions. At risk of beating our own drum, the revised boots performed wonderfully during our four-month polar trek. Although we found them a trifle heavier than usual, we never suffered a single blister and felt no hint of frostbite, even when the temperature fell to $-50°C$ ($-58°F$). To cap its sponsorship, Kaufman also provided us with $50,000.

But even before Kaufman came aboard, Alcatel (then known as Canada Wire and Cable) had demonstrated its support. It was the first large firm that got behind our project, even though it didn't stand to benefit directly; we weren't using any of its products. Peter Green, then its president, had been introduced to us by John Mordhorst, who'd met Green when a number of Alcatel staff members attended an Outward Bound course. Our preliminary meeting took place in Green's office in downtown Toronto. Richard, John, Bob, and Liane Benoit (our expedition manager) arrived there filled with timidity. At this point, the

Weber–Malakhov balance sheet read precisely zero. Green listened politely to our pitch, then promised a cheque for $30,000, later raised to $50,000. The four supplicants walked somewhat dazedly to an elevator, waited for the doors to close, and spontaneously began to jump up and down, whooping and shouting for joy. With the stroke of Green's pen, our project had achieved fiscal respectability.

So much for Canadian capitalism. Meanwhile, Misha had also been shaking the funding tree. The Ryazan Machine Tool Manufacturing Amalgamation had sponsored him during Icewalk, and he once again contacted Anatoliy Semenovich, the firm's general director. By this time – the end of 1991 – the machine-tool plant, like everything else in Russia, was making an often painful transition to a free-market economy. Mindful of this fact, Misha had dared to hope only for an airline ticket to Canada. Semenovich took one look at him and asked, "Are you going on another journey?" Misha nodded, and Semenovich said, "I think it's my duty to help my fellow townsman. Will $15,000 Canadian suit you?" With that, the expedition's bi-national fiscal basis was safe and sound.

As we've said, the complexities of a polar attempt demand a full-time manager. Late in 1991, Richard had been at the Banff Festival of Mountain Films, regaling audiences with his experiences during Polar Bridge. After he'd spoken, he was passed a note with a telephone number and the name Liane Benoit. By chance, Liane had met his mother and learned about our upcoming journey. She was an able cyclist and cross-country skier who'd also had experience in the public-relations field. She quickly joined the team, along with Richard's wife, Josée, who'd already volunteered her services as treasurer, recording secretary, and seamstress-in-charge. In fact, the entire Weber clan was quick to gather round. Richard's father, Hans, was of enormous help. He is a noted scientist with a lifetime's experience in glaciology and

geophysics, the study of Arctic ice patterns and underwater land
formations. And so, with the final addition of Jean Castonguay
and Vasiliy Zaushitsyn, who would serve as our radio links to
Canada and Russia, the team was complete, and we could begin
to fine-tune our plans.

Our departure from Ward Hunt Island was slated for February 23, 1992. Our timetable suggested that, if we experienced no
undue delays, we would return ninety-eight days later, on or
about the end of the first week of June. We presumed that the ice
conditions would enable us to do so – that is, the ice wouldn't
break up and strand us offshore on our way back. In 1988, Polar
Bridge arrived at Ward Hunt on June 1, with little difficulty.
Nothing is more unpredictable than Arctic ice, but the statistical
probabilities were on our side.

Next we turned our attention to clothing and food. Our trip
would be in effect an extended marathon. We did not fear the
cold; we knew how to defend ourselves against it, but we knew
also that we'd face a constant battle to maintain our physical
strength. Our clothing would be the first line of defence. You can
survive in the Arctic wearing almost anything – witness the early
explorers, who dressed like escapees from a lunatic asylum but
didn't die. The trick is not to waste energy just keeping warm.
Survival has to be second nature; you don't have time to make
plans from scratch. As Misha says, "You get a little bit stupid out
there." You have to function in a machinelike way, and the
machine must be adequately fuelled. Proper diet and ample rest
were absolutely vital. If we began to weaken, our systems would
direct their energies to the physical work at hand and cease to
warm our bodies. Misha stressed over and over again the need for
a balanced daily ration, and we finally settled on 1.2 kilograms
(2.6 lb.) of food per man per day. Our basic diet was breakfast:
instant oats, ground nuts, whole powdered milk, a small amount
of raisins, and instant coffee; lunch: double-smoked bacon, dry

sausage, nuts, chocolate, pilote biscuits, butter; supper: pasta or rice, pemmican, freeze-dried cheese and sour cream, herbal tea. No vegetables or fruit or anything green, so multivitamins supplied by our sponsor Shaklee were essential. Scurvy has its onset in about two months. . . . After four months one would no doubt be dead.

Each of us would consume – and burn – an extraordinary 7,000 calories daily, which gives some idea of the intensity of our efforts. That much food translates also as a great deal of weight to drag across the ice, but the alternative held no appeal. In 1989-90, a Russian expedition lost one of its members to what was rather guardedly described as "coronary deficiency." The following year, another man developed an ulcer and bled to death. Misha believes that the first victim succumbed to common dystrophy. The group's daily food ration was only 800 grams (28 oz.) per man – not nearly enough to sustain the team's hard labours on the ice.

Other than food, our last-minute discussions focused on minor points. For example, we debated endlessly exactly what defined an "unsupported" expedition. This might strike an observer as hair-splitting in the extreme, but such thoughts are paramount in the Arctic explorer's mind. Once you commit yourself to press on without resupply, there are very strict protocols to be observed. For example, during Steger's expedition, a plane arrived to evacuate Bob Mantell, who was suffering from frostbite. The pilot offered coffee to the other members of the group, but they refused, because this would have constituted "resupply." At another point, when the marchers had almost reached the Pole, they began to experience trouble with their sextant. There was no question that they'd reach their goal, but they literally didn't know which way to turn. A military plane was flying overhead and established radio contact. The pilot asked how they were getting along. They admitted that they were having one or two problems and asked for a check on their coordinates. The

pilot refused, stating that their base-camp manager had speci-
fically instructed him not to reveal such information. Fortunately,
they got straightened away — but the incident shows how seriously the ground rules, once established, must be adhered to, even
in the slightest particular.

In any case, Richard argued that we should take along a
sextant to determine our coordinates, if only as a backup to our
other navigational devices, which included a Global Positioning
System (GPS). The GPS is a wonderful thing — a marvel of
modern technology. The battery-powered transmitter/receiver
is about the size of a TV remote control. It beams your location
to a system of deep-space satellites, then tells you exactly where
you are. In 1989, the device (which has since been modified and
isn't quite so precise) could register movement in steps. If you
took a couple of giant strides in one direction or another, your
position would read back differently. As well as the GPS, we were
to carry, as our links to the outside world, a radio and two TUBSAT
transmitter/receivers (described later).

At one point, Richard thought seriously about dispensing with
the GPS altogether. Misha, however, thought it unwise to leave it
behind. "If we were to follow your logic," he said, "we should sew
clothing of caribou skins, which we have thankfully decided not
to do. Perhaps you also want to take a club and run along with it
to catch a polar bear. I do not wish to do that either. GPS is not an
outside support; it is a means to help us confirm where we are.
This is the twentieth century. Our expedition will acknowledge
that fact, and be natural in its own way, true to our own time. We
choose for the trip the very best that is available in the modern
world. Robert Scott and Fridtjof Nansen took advantage of the
latest inventions of their era. For heaven's sake, let us not go to
extremes." But to only partial avail! Richard indeed took along a
sextant weighing several kilograms — strange in an era when we
communicated with each other via E-mail. Misha arrived in

Canada by non-stop jet, and the whole expedition, rather than inching its way north by sailing ship, flew lock, stock, and overflowing packing cases to Iqaluit in January 1992.

CHAPTER THREE

Iqaluit, Baffin Island, Northwest Territories, lies on the shore of Frobisher Bay – the town's name for many years. Hills surround it on every side. The waters of the bay register twelve-metre (40-ft.) tides – the second highest in the world – and are full of treacherous currents that contort the surface, forming ridges of broken ice that resemble their pressure-ridge big brothers. It's a bit of an oversimplification, but the bay could be said to represent the Arctic in miniature – with one notable exception. Out on the ocean, there's nowhere to escape to, whereas in Iqaluit, you can train in conditions that approximate those you'll face en route and then return to a warm room in a civilized dwelling. It doesn't feel a bit like the back of beyond; there are several shops, restaurants, and hotels. Direct flights leave daily for Ottawa and Montreal; if you've forgotten something, it's easy enough to order it up. Will Steger was the first to use Iqaluit as a training ground, and we'd come to know it well while training for Polar Bridge. Our friend Brent Boddy had settled down there, and it was nice to spend time with him, talking over old experiences. Plus it offered at least some sunlight, even in January, as opposed to Resolute Bay farther north, which was then locked firmly in the polar night. Now we enjoyed its hospitality once again, as the final training trips, meetings, and negotiations took place. Here was where our expedition really began. The dated entries that follow are based on the detailed diaries we both kept, to record the day-by-day countdown to our departure from Ward Hunt and the expedition itself once it was under way.

FEBRUARY 3. We awoke this morning to a snowstorm. The hills to the north were covered by a greyish haze that lingered despite the biting wind. John suggested that we stay indoors and rest, but we knew that he sought only to postpone the inevitable. Now was the time to confront the weather, which would surely worsen before we were done. We had to dispel our doubts at once; out on the drifting ice, it would be too late. We exchanged glances, and Misha would remember John's comment as the first sign of impending trouble, but nothing was said aloud.

Over breakfast we debated another problem, which may sound rather ridiculous — whether we were dressed too warmly. In fact, a polar traveller's main enemy is humidity, not cold *per se*. We would sweat profusely while dragging our heavy loads, and our clothing would become soaked, then freeze into a useless mass. The same held true for our sleeping bags, boots, and tent. The equipment can breathe, or it can be waterproof, but it can't be both ways. This was the age-old Arctic paradox: walking in $-50°C$ $(-58°F)$ temperatures while fretting over a possible surplus of heat. Of course, we ought not to feel the cold, and flimsy clothing would not suffice. We had designed our wardrobe with this in mind — inner and outer layers that could be taken off and put on as the need arose. Bob, however, was not disposed to follow our example. He didn't reveal his choice of an outfit until just before we were to set off. In fact, he didn't need his full polar suit while in Iqaluit, even though it was $-40°C$ $(-40°F)$. That sounds cold enough, but it's nothing compared with the very same temperature out on the Arctic Ocean, where it's darker and much more humid. Nor had he taken his full kit to the earlier training sessions on Baffin Island. When Misha finally got a look at it, he was appalled: apart from the boots, it was the same gear in which Bob had frozen to the bone during Steger's expedition – a thin nylon anorak and woollen sweater and pants. Granted, Bob's problem in 1986 had been severe frostbite to his feet, but that was a result of the fact that his entire wardrobe was inadequate; he simply couldn't keep warm enough.

Misha tried to sway Bob by citing the words of Vladimir Rakhmanov, a member of the *Komsomolskaya Pravda* team: "Nobody has ever found roasted people in the Arctic, but frostbitten ones, in abundance." Richard had laughed his head off upon first hearing this gem of folk wisdom, but neither of us was laughing now. We mounted other, more serious arguments as well, but Bob refused to modify his gear.

FEBRUARY 6. We made two shuttle trips today, pulling about ninety kilograms (198 lb.) each, and made camp out on the frozen bay, not far from the airport's flight path. It seemed to take us an eternity to do something as simple as pitching the tent. This was the first time that we'd attempted to function as a team, as Misha hadn't been present during the early training runs. We hadn't yet defined or assumed our individual duties.

FEBRUARY 12. Bob and John continued to wrestle with their gear. Both of them had brought fibreglass and Kevlar sleds that measured at least three metres (10 ft.) long. They looked suitably imposing, and in fact worked reasonably well at first, but soon one of them developed a nasty crack. They seemed to us unwieldy, unstable, and uncomfortable. Misha especially was a strong opponent of large sleds: he'd seen how his Russian cohorts (who insisted on the biggest, most old-fashioned sleds they could lay their hands on) had come to grief amid the polar ice. Even worse, Bob had also built himself not one but two wooden komatiks. The komatik is a traditional Inuit sled – but the Inuit wisely choose to hitch it to a team of dogs. Bob's komatiks worked relatively well in Iqaluit, which made it hard to prove that they would not do well on the ocean, but how he would fare when the going got rough was past imagining. They resembled pieces of patio furniture — wooden *chaise longues*, mounted on wooden runners. But Bob declared that he would pull at least one of them, along with one of the big synthetic sleds. John opted for one large and two small plastic sleds, plus a backpack. Both Richard and Misha took two small sleds (the famous Norcaboggans), plus two backpacks. Even the small sleds weighed in excess of sixty kilograms (132 lb.) each fully loaded — a load we approximated with sandbags during our training runs.

Even among the miniature ridges of the bay, it soon became apparent that Bob's komatiks were difficult to control. They bumped against the ridges and threatened to overturn; he had to strain to pull them free of the smallest depression in the ice. On a downhill slope, they behaved like runaway trucks; you had to jump aside or they'd catch up with you and mow you down. We tried to pull one and found that it strained our backs, but Bob was adamant, and we had to let him be.

FEBRUARY 12. Back at the tent, Misha busied himself with a number of control experiments. First he set out to determine how much fuel would be required to dry our sleeping bags. In April we could put them outdoors in the sun, but until then we'd have to dry them inside the tent, consuming precious fuel. The human body releases at least half a litre (18 fl. oz.) of water overnight, so he began by trying to pour a full litre (35 fl. oz.) into the bag's interior. It wouldn't take that amount, and he had to settle for 800 grams (28 oz.). Thus a bag would serve only for one or two days. He left the test bag rolled up and let it freeze overnight. The next morning, the experiment continued, but once again yielded unfavourable results. All three stoves, burning at full tilt for an hour, evaporated only 300 grams (11 oz.) of water, meanwhile consuming 600 millilitres (21 fl. oz.) of fuel. This wouldn't do, and we were left with three possible courses of action: look for a bag of higher quality (it didn't exist); hope that we could put up with excess moisture in our bags for the first part of our journey (a disagreeable prospect at best); or take two bags each, then throw one away.

The second experiment determined how many candles we'd need to light our tent in the morning and evening hours. They would be our sole source of illumination; we hadn't packed a gas or battery-powered lantern. The candles burned at a rate of thirty millimetres (1.2 in.) per hour. Each candle measured 120 millimetres (4.7 in.). Thus, each would provide a mere four hours of light. We'd want two candles at a time, burning for two hours every morning and evening. Each candle weighed thirty grams (1 oz.), so our daily ration equalled sixty grams (2 oz.). Multiplied by thirty (the number of totally or primarily pitch-dark days we'd encounter en route), the total weight came to 1.8 kilograms (3.9 lb.). Misha studied a table of the light-times (including morning and evening twilight) between Ward Hunt and the Pole and decreed that we'd take enough candles to last us for two weeks only – a total of 900 grams (31.7 oz.).

FEBRUARY 13. We had agreed the night before to begin training each day at 9 A.M. But over breakfast, John called us together and expressed dissatisfaction with the way our preparations were going. "Nothing ever goes according to plan," he said. "At first we agreed to start at eight o'clock, and we should stick to that, even though we have to get up an hour earlier. We're all over the map; we don't know what to rely on from one day to another. The training period is going to be extended indefinitely."

He had a point, and that day we made several marches, erected the tent, had supper, sat around the stoves, dried our clothes, and went to sleep. John's complaints echoed in our minds as we lay in our bags. A period of adaptation is always difficult. Each of us was an experienced traveller in his own right, each with his own outlook and preconceptions. Misha considered but rejected the idea of attempting to assume a greater leadership role. He knew that his experiences had been primarily with Russian expeditions, which were larger, more regimented groups. Now he was feeling his way and did not wish to act precipitously, even though John's and especially Bob's behaviour struck him as inappropriate. Misha was confident that Richard had the situation in hand. He'd trained with Bob and John; he knew them better, and it was unwise for Misha to be heavy-handed or intrusive.

FEBRUARY 14. This morning John was the bearer of far more unwelcome news. "Guys," he said, "I've got a serious question: Do you think you could do the expedition as a group of three? All of a sudden, it hit me — the kind of hardships we're going to face up there. I've been thinking back to the training trips on Baffin Island — how hard it was, the day-in, day-out grind. I've been wondering why I want to do this trip, and I can't find an answer. There's a sense of futility; I just don't know what the meaning is anymore. I have serious doubts, and I've decided to confide in you now, before it's too late."

   Bob muttered something along the lines of "We'll miss you." But Misha, although taken aback, had sufficient presence of mind to take the right tack. "You're right," he said. "It isn't pleasant to travel under these conditions. I can tell you sincerely that the greatest pleasure you'll feel is when you come home and recall how it was during the journey. One has to suffer all the time, so your doubts are understandable. And if you truly believe that you aren't ready or willing to go with us, then your decision is correct. It's far more courageous to admit your doubts now than for you to start off without believing fully in your strength. Sooner or later it would have become obvious that you were unwilling to go on, but by then it would be impossible to correct your mistake. But don't be hasty; think it over for the rest of the day, and let's talk again this evening."

Throughout the day, we made only two marches instead of our scheduled three. We couldn't believe at first that John would leave the expedition — but as the day wore on, we began to realize that chances were there'd be only the three of us left.

FEBRUARY 17. This evening John announced his final decision: he would not take part in the journey. This came as no surprise. After his initial confession yesterday, he seemed to withdraw from us, although he kept on helping out as best he could.

Our next step was to contact Peter Green, at Alcatel, who after all had been introduced to us by John. As a major sponsor, he had the right to be kept informed of such a significant alteration in our plans. Green listened carefully (and was probably as shocked as we were), but his support was unwavering. "If the three of you propose to endure the journey, then you must go on," he said.

FEBRUARY 18. We made eight trial marches amid very cold temperatures and fifty kilometre-per-hour (31 mph) winds. Perhaps we're trying to make the best of the inevitable, but the atmosphere in our tent seems to have improved since John's announcement. He is by nature an individualist; he's touchy and sometimes takes offense at mere trifles. In the confined quarters of a polar expedition, this sort of reaction could only exacerbate the stress, which will be ample, even under optimum circumstances. Oddly, Misha has decided that he "knew it all along." He claims that he expected that John would not continue, and this may very well be so. He has the ability to get an instant fix on people's basic natures and intentions. Perhaps when his polar career is done, he can set up shop with a deck of tarot cards; the world would beat a path to his door in Ryazan.

FEBRUARY 21. Today Josée arrived with Tessum and Nansen, the Weber family's sons. Richard went shopping for presents, and everyone joined in the last-minute packing.

FEBRUARY 25. Josée has been followed up here by members of our film crew, and by Liane Benoit, who looked tired and drawn. She pounced on Misha, accusing him first of a watchful and untrusting attitude towards her. She then accused him of driving John away, if only by denying him the chance to demonstrate his capabilities. Next she accused Richard and Bob of allowing John to learn about Misha's low opinion of him. This is not the sort of thing we wish to hear from our expedition manager, and it produces nothing but an atmosphere of real, not imagined, watchfulness and distrust.

But, looking back, we realized that John had had doubts for quite some time. During one of our earliest training sessions, Misha had unexpectedly grabbed a videocamera and asked everyone to say a few words about the upcoming trip. Only John refused to speak for the record. It seemed curious at the time — but now, in retrospect, it seems to indicate that even then his mind was uneasy about the whole affair.

That's why it was doubly strange when, this very night, our film crew asked us to re-enact the conversation during which John first admitted his doubts. We all trooped obediently out onto the ice and sat inside the tent. We aren't actors; we had difficulty remembering our lines. In fact, we had a sense of weird unreality, as if we were indeed actors, or as if the whole thing was happening to someone else. Then, on cue, John stepped through the tent flap, and repeated, "Guys, I've got a serious question. . . ."

FEBRUARY 26. John left today, and we parted warmly. He mustn't be blamed for his decision; he simply understood that the trial was not for him. He did not run away, but made a practical estimation of his own strength and acted upon it wisely.

In fact, we're far more worried these days about Bob, who insists on sticking to his own concepts of clothing and nutrition, which Misha in particular finds wildly unsuitable. Food is the key to physical performance in an extreme climate; you'd better know exactly what you're eating, and why. For example, each morning and evening we'll eat as a group, served from a communal pot. But to add variety, each of us is free to choose what he wishes for lunch (which we define as a series of snacks throughout the working day). The only condition that Misha, in his role as consulting physician, insisted on was that lunch be rich in calories.

Perhaps Bob's choice is grounded in his previous experiences, or maybe he simply likes seafood. At any rate, he's gone overboard on sardines — swimming in oil and packed in heavy tins — and on biscuits whose nutritive value Richard compared to eating air. Misha inspected Bob's larder and lost his temper. "Where are your calories?" he shouted. "We both have forty-two kilograms (93 lb.) of lunch foods, but your lunches will provide you with three, maybe four hundred calories fewer than mine each day. Don't you see what that means? Every day you'll be weaker than me by that exact amount. You'll fall behind by one or two marches; you won't be able to do the work." But Bob would not heed Misha's advice. He replied that everything would be all right, which it certainly was not, even at that time. He had no plan; he didn't know what he'd be eating from one day to another.

Stymied in his efforts to make Bob see the light, Misha began to quarrel with Liane. It seemed to him that she hadn't coped with the volume of work at hand. Liane was offended, claimed that she'd been working night and day, and announced that she, too, was leaving the expedition. Richard grew upset, Misha calmed him down, and Liane changed her mind and agreed to stay. But our arguments continued. Some centred on the question of who held a share in the expedition – that is, who would profit if it eventually made money and who would be held liable for any debts and shortfalls. We'd planned to incorporate the expedition, and Liane wanted to be an equal member. Misha objected to this, and Josée, who'd been primarily responsible for the finances thus far, had several concerns of her own, which she did not hesitate to make plain, rather more cogently than did Liane. This was a difficult period, and some of the more contentious issues remained unresolved – largely because it was almost time to leave Iqaluit and make our way to Ward Hunt.

FEBRUARY 28. Today we made preparations for a farewell dinner – a way of saying thanks to all the friends who'd helped us while in Iqaluit, including Larry Horlick, Ken MacRury, Jane Cooper, Bronyk Skavinsky, Brent Boddy, and the staff of First Air.

FEBRUARY 29. Overnight a storm blew up, blocking the streets and imprisoning us indoors. We cancelled all our visits, issued IOUs for the dinner party, and kept busy with a myriad last-minute details, double- and triple-checking our gear. Initially, the start date was to have been February 23. The pilots of the charter airplanes would not land at Ward Hunt before March 3, however, because there was not enough light. To land earlier, they needed someone on the ground to mark and light an airstrip.

MARCH 3. The storm abated and we could fly northward. Surely we couldn't have forgotten anything, but we continued to fret over our supplies until the final moments prior to departure. Richard said goodbye to his family at the airport. It's always difficult to part with your loved ones; his eldest son, Tessum, clung to him and cried. Tessum knew only that Richard was going on a long trip and would "ski, live in a tent, and eat cheese." Misha was oddly glad that his wife, Olga, and their children, Misha, Jr., and Aloysha, were far away. It would have hurt him to feel as Richard felt; absence was hard enough, but perhaps the easiest way. Richard took a window seat aboard the plane, staring down at the endless white spaces that appeared beneath its wings, but seemed to see nothing at all.

MARCH 4. We landed in Resolute and met with Vasiliy and Jean, our radio operators. Vasiliy quickly secured a link with Ryazan, and Misha spoke with Olga, who said that life went on; their kids were doing their early-morning exercises with a set of dumbbells — a touch of blessed normalcy. We splurged, spending thirty-five dollars a head on dinner at the Narwhal Hotel, and met with Martin Williams, a Canadian adventurer, and two Norwegians who were about to set off on a one-way supported expedition. Their attitude made it plain that they understood the difference between our journeys; they seemed almost to hold us in awe. On the other hand, perhaps they thought that they would never again see us alive.

MARCH 5. Aboard the plane to Eureka — a Canadian government high-Arctic weather station and necessary refuelling stop — then onward to Ward Hunt, as ice fields appeared beneath the Twin Otter's wings. Ellesmere Island's mountains came into view — magnificent peaks, shrouded in low-hanging clouds. At about 1 P.M. we were ready to make our approach, but asked the pilot to detour to the north so that we could estimate the condition of the ice. Then we circled above the island and jolted down onto the makeshift landing strip, which had been blown almost clear by the wind, exposing rough gravel beneath the snow — not what you wish to hit at speed when the aircraft has skis, not wheels, as landing gear. We began to remove our equipment while the crew marked out a smoother surface on the ice for their take-off. Within an hour, they were gone, leaving us alone on the deserted shore.

CHAPTER FOUR

The Twin Otter forced its way through a screen of sullen grey clouds and disappeared. In a moment, the sound of its engines had faded from the sky. Now we had left the civilized world behind us. Home, family, and the coming of spring were suddenly remote from our existence. Ahead lay nothing but uncertainty and unnamed peril all along the arduous route we'd dreamt of for so long.

Richard surveyed the desolate vista and said with unusual sentimentality, "Two and a half years of fighting and worry! Now at last we have a real task in front of us."

But our first duty was mundane in the extreme: we had to excavate our new home, a snow-covered hut measuring five metres by seven metres (16 ft. × 23 ft.). Ward Hunt had been a military training base during the 1950s, and a fair bit of junk remains; a derelict bulldozer sits off to one side, along with the usual complement of oil drums. Next to the hut is a second, even more dilapidated structure that had been relegated to the position of a storehouse. Ironically, it was almost completely free of snow — but to force an entry into our temporary abode, we had to rummage like moles for at least an hour through two-metre (7-ft.) drifts, looking in vain for the door.

Eventually, the entranceway appeared, and we stepped inside. The snow had preceded us; smaller drifts had piled up along the floorboards. Everything bore a stamp of abandonment and disuse. The previous occupant had been Ranulph Fiennes, several years before, but, in the meantime, a fox had managed to squeeze in through one of the cracks and leave tracks all over a bed.

We quickly put our dwelling place in order. Bob fired up the stove, and the hut became reasonably warm, except at floor level, where the temperature remained well below zero. Amid these rustic surroundings, we bedded down for our first night on the shore of the Arctic Ocean.

MARCH 8. In two days we've managed to carry most of our load across the ice shelf and out to the first range of pressure ridges. But they don't intimidate us; we know them well. To us, they're like rapids during a canoe trip — you paddle the calm stretches just to reach the next set and get your blood racing again. Yesterday we made three marches of forty-five minutes each. Our progress is slowed by the fact that Bob will not be parted from his remaining komatik. At least he agreed to leave one of them behind in Iqaluit, in favour of two smaller sleds like ours. Fully loaded, it weighs well over 100 kilograms (220 lb.) — an impossible burden. Bob trudges along, leaning forward at a constant forty-five-degree angle into the wind. At times he is bent almost parallel to the ground. The weight is beyond his powers; on a downhill slope, the komatik becomes a sort of mobile battering ram.

This evening Misha goes out of his way to encourage Bob, making sure to congratulate him on his progress. We must support him whenever we can; we'll all have to depend on one another if we're to accomplish our aims. If only we could persuade him to have done with his komatik! But he is supremely obstinate and ignores even Misha's praise. He never enters into a group discussion or bothers to defend his actions — he merely goes ahead and does what he wants. He doesn't like our choice of clothing? No problem! He simply puts on his own, no matter how inappropriate. He wants to take more fuel? He commandeers an extra twelve litres (3 gal.), and stows it in his already overloaded komatik. This drives Misha wild: every drop of "excess" fuel confounds his calculations. He fears that it will slow our progress even more and suspects that Bob's desire for creature comforts may indicate further weakness. In Misha's words, "Warmth is just a sensation." Perhaps Bob is still reacting to his unsuccessful journey of 1986 and is trying to assert himself, to cheer himself by making unilateral decisions. But he forges ahead without complaint, and perhaps we are overreacting. A dash of obstinacy, after all, will come in handy along the way.

Today we caught a momentary glimpse of the sun for the first time in almost a week. It appeared behind the hut and looked so very beautiful.

MARCH 8. Today's marches proved to be somewhat easier. Bob walked surprisingly quickly, and we crossed the ice shelf in far less time than we'd taken the day before. We were aided by the wind, which had blown away the soft snow overnight. Inspired by our success, we began to lug the first part of our load out onto the ocean itself.

Easier said than done. The first range of pressure ridges is one of the very worst between us and the Pole – a consequence of the fact that the ice shelf is fixed, a virtual extension of the shoreline. It doesn't give under the impact of the pack ice, and the only way that the broken ice can bulge is up. We walk to and fro, looking for a corridor that will enable us to pull our sleds.

MARCH 9. We are stranded inside the hut, waiting out a storm. The wind has changed, bringing with it heavy clouds and heavier snow. The air is dark, and, were we on the ice, we could not see our hands in front of our faces. We pace back and forth within our cramped prison, cursing the elements. From time to time, one of us ventures outside, but even a breath of fresh air brings no pleasure or release.

Richard cannot stay still. His first project was to salvage and repair two abandoned wind generators, and now we have electricity. Besides light, the devices provide us with useful information: we can measure the force of the wind without opening the door, simply by glancing at the amperage meter. A reading of five amperes means a very strong gust indeed; but despite the wind, the hut has remained cosy enough during the day. During the night, however, the rising wind sucked out any accumulated warmth. Richard grumbled and sprang into action, plunging outside to plug the gaps with snow. Then he did the rounds of the interior walls, searching for holes and crevices. He is, after all, a mechanical engineer by training; his technical cast of mind prohibits him from tolerating even the slightest disorder.

Then, having rendered the hut virtually airtight, he went in search of new activities. Another delight in this dull grey world is a shopping spree. He decided to see what Fiennes had left us in the storehouse next door. The more food we can forage, the less of our own we'll have to consume while we engage in this interminable waiting.

Richard sampled the shopping list, item by item. The tinned crab meat is good; the lobster bisque, okay, as is the Irish stew. The tinned milk and (tinned!) steak-and-kidney pie have seen better days. We found a trove of honey, jam, and butter in a large aluminum box, along with a good selection of oversize chocolate bars, each one marked with a twenty-five-cent price tag. So much for the ravages of inflation! But Fiennes, true to his upbringing, had also brought along that traditional standby of the British Empire — tins of boiled sweets. We pocketed some; they will serve as welcome treats along the way.

Next, Richard — now turned master chef — concocted his recipe for Mashed Potatoes à la Ward Hunt: dissolve the freeze-dried spuds in boiling water, adding pepper and ersatz cheese spread. Stir and consume in five minutes flat, garnishing with a

dash of frosty air and freshly fallen snow, and follow it up with
tinned pears for dessert.

We are bored. Forced idleness weighs upon our minds; each
day in this claustrophobic limbo means a day behind schedule on
the ice.

MARCH 12. The wind is stronger still. The storm rages day and
night; there seems to be no end to it. Bob is asleep — a lucky man,
because in his dreams he cannot dwell on the passing time.
Richard skims through the local library — too elegant a word for
a pile of outdated books and magazines. The hut has become, if
not a prison, then very like a doctor's waiting room. Misha, our
real-life physician, is broadening his vocabulary. He has discovered an issue of *Penthouse Forum*, but must pause every other para-
graph to check unfamiliar verbs in a dictionary. Then he tosses
the learning tools aside and begins to brood on dire scenarios.
What awaits us on the ice? Will storms of this magnitude be the
norm this season? How many more days will be lost in fruitless
waiting? Will the snow bury the partial load we've left on the ice,
or will we be able to locate it when the weather breaks?

Five days have passed, with not a single step forward. The
Arctic has shut the door in our faces — we can imagine its compla-
cent and mocking smile. It will decide when to admit us into its
icy realm.

How tiresomely the time is crawling! Even our radio contacts
bring no good news. Our friends in Ottawa and Resolute, in
Moscow and Ryazan, cannot understand why we haven't got
underway. Liane suspects, for some reason, that Bob is ill. In fact,
all three of us are literally under the weather and can do nothing
about it. But sooner or later, the storm must moderate, and we
will be able to set off. Indeed, late in the day, Richard stepped
outside and reported that although the wind was even stronger,

the visibility had marginally increased. A positive sign; perhaps it means that we can make a start tomorrow.

MARCH 13 (EXPEDITION DAY ONE). We are in our sleeping bags, out on the ocean ice. At six o'clock this morning, the storm still raged. Then, two hours later, everything was dead calm, the snow stopped falling, and Cape Columbia could be clearly seen in the distance. We feverishly packed and at 2 P.M. said goodbye to the snowbound hut.

Within an hour we reached the edge of the ice shelf, where five days ago we'd left part of our load. But absolutely nothing could be seen. We poked hopefully at a huge drift, which proved to be Bob's komatik. The smaller sleds were far more difficult to locate. Feeling more like archaeologists than polar explorers, we probed with our ski poles until we struck a solid object below. Then we used our shovels to uncover the sleds beneath snow that had accumulated half a metre (2 ft.) deep. Next we crossed the first range of pressure ridges and found the second part of our load. Luckily, it was covered with much less snow and proved far more easy to spot. Here we decided to make our camp for the night.

Soon it will be midnight, and we long for sleep. Tomorrow the real work begins.

CHAPTER FIVE

MARCH 14 (DAY TWO). We are slowed by minor mishaps. This morning the kettle started to leak. Richard had left it filled with water, which froze, expanded, and fractured the bottom seal. He patched it with thermal glue, but Misha doubted that the repair would hold and skied all the way back to the hut to fetch a replacement pot, thus wasting, in Richard's estimation, a precious two and a half hours. (Richard's handiwork would be vindicated. The repair held, but the spare pot came in handy when our equipment had to be redivided, as we shall see.)

MARCH 15 (DAY THREE). Slow progress, although Bob agreed to abandon six litres (1 gal.) of spare fuel, along with several other items. His komatik continues to impede us; he lags almost fifteen minutes behind the pace.

MARCH 16 (DAY FOUR). Another storm descends, forcing us to build a snow wall around the tent to cut the wind. We have had only two clear days since our arrival on Ward Hunt. This is beastly weather; where are the fabled Arctic high-pressure zones when we need them? Misha decides to barbecue his ration of bacon, chopping it into small chunks and, speared on his Swiss Army knife, holding them over one of the stoves, as if toasting marshmallows.

MARCH 17 (DAY FIVE). It snows again — a total of at least twenty centimetres (8 in.), counting yesterday. The flakes are large and fluffy; they remind Richard of Christmas in Ottawa. But they bode no good, and our progress continues to be maddeningly slow.

MARCH 19 (DAY SEVEN). More snow, which buried Bob's komatik up to the handlebars overnight. During one march, Misha noticed that a warning sticker had fallen off one of the Norcaboggans as it bounced across a pressure ridge. He studied it and announced that the sled was intended for use "only in areas free of obstacles and well away from cars." One out of two ain't bad; if only the sled's designers could see us now.

MARCH 21 (DAY NINE). Today we made three classic shuttle marches, moving forward an hour at a time. Returning takes less than half that time; we've begun to fall into a productive rhythm. We do well with our sleds, but Bob, burdened with his komatik, confessed that he'd had enough for the day. Richard doled out some of Fiennes's boiled sweets – a small reward for such hard labour, but small rewards will help sustain our efforts. Our mood is more upbeat; we feel that now that we're finally in motion, we need only a modicum of good luck. Its appearance is long overdue, and we ask so little of fortune.

Richard received news from home via radio: Tessum, on holidays from school, was driving a dogsled; and Nansen, the younger child, had taken his first steps.

MARCH 23 (DAY ELEVEN). The usual routine, although Bob seems somewhat more tired. He does not talk or smile. But he is moving well, despite his outrageous load.

MARCH 25 (DAY THIRTEEN). During the rest period after our second march, our teeth were chattering with cold. Richard set off on the next march at a furious pace, trying to warm himself, and Misha had to struggle to keep up. Suddenly, he thought of an old joke concerning Roald Amundsen's dogs. Tired of their human burden, one said to another, "This is a heavy weight. Why drag him all the way to the Pole? Let's eat him now." "No," said the second dog. "Let him freeze. When we get to the Pole, we'll thaw him out and enjoy him all the more."

MARCH 26 (DAY FOURTEEN). Today we considered making a larger number of shorter shuttle marches – half an hour each, as opposed to an hour. We had encountered a bad patch of pressure ridges that tired us out. We managed to squeeze our way through the ice rubble, but Bob's komatik kept getting wedged between obstacles and stuck in the broken ice. Even with all three of us pushing and pulling by turns, it constantly got hung up or bogged down. We desperately wish that Bob would realize how counterproductive the komatik has become, but he must reach this conclusion himself; we cannot impose our will or dictate to him. The wind is most unpleasant today, and the temperature, −37°C (−35°F). The tip of Richard's nose is frostbitten, as is Bob's, but Misha thus far remains unaffected.

MARCH 27 (DAY FIFTEEN). Misha awoke at 7 A.M. and tried to rouse us with a cheerful good morning. Silence reigned, but, ten minutes later, Bob stirred and suggested that we could afford to sleep in. Later, over breakfast, he began to talk about a full day's rest. While drinking our coffee, we debated his proposal. The temperature remained at −35°C (−31°F), and the wind was up. The past few days had been very hard on us, even with the shortened marches. We agreed to stop for the day and figure out exactly where we were.

Bob, the designated navigator, went outside with his trusty sextant, busied himself for a considerable time, and announced that we had reached 83°28′ — scant progress, despite our best efforts. Richard took out a notebook and began to calculate our average speed. Over thirty-one marches, we had made only 0.65 miles (1.2 km) per hour — about half the rate we'd expected.

Each of us hoped that Bob had made a mistake in his readings. To check them, we would have to switch on the GPS — which Richard had initially argued against. But he himself took out the device, warmed the batteries, and turned it on. The figures flashed an instant reply: 83°30′. Bob's antediluvian sextant had been a mere two minutes off — an infinitesimal error that meant only that our average speed was in fact 0.8 miles (1.5 km) per hour. At least Richard was now convinced of the need to use the most efficient methods to navigate, that is, with the GPS, and not waste time with the sextant. In future we would use the GPS at every opportunity and wouldn't have to stand outside, searching for the sun in a cloudy sky and sweating over arcane tables for three-quarters of an hour at a time.

How could we manage to march more quickly? Obviously, Bob would have to drop his komatik. We argued with him throughout the day, pointing out that the first half of each shuttle march (when everybody pulled only the small sleds) went much faster than the second half, even though we were slogging through fresh snow. The second half of each march, despite the fact that we had a trail to follow, went far more slowly, because of the komatik. But Bob remained impervious to our pleadings. Sooner or later, we will have to issue an ultimatum, even though we cannot foresee the result.

To leaven our humdrum existence, Richard once again played chef, augmenting a package of soup from Fiennes's supply with sausages and bacon – scarcely *nouvelle cuisine*. But that is what a day of rest entails – sleep, meals, and desultory conversation. Bob remained uncommunicative and withdrawn, so we fell to discussing absent friends and the occasional enemy. Barely two weeks have passed, but already we feel isolated from the world beyond. Only our sporadic radio communications inform us that we are not alone in the high Arctic. Today Jean has kept us abreast of the progress being made by two other expeditions. A party of Norwegians is making its way from Russia and has crossed 83° on that side of the Pole, with a view to continuing all the way across to Canada. Basically, its members are retracing the path taken by Polar Bridge – but they, like us, are travelling unsupported. (Unfortunately, one of them would fall ill and have to be taken out by helicopter. Later he rejoined the expedition by parachuting onto the ice.) Well, they aren't doing too badly thus far. Martin Williams and the two Norwegians we'd met in Resolute are slightly ahead of us. They have managed to get past 84° and

are sure to precede us to the Pole. But theirs, as we've said, is a
one-way supported journey only, and no cause for concern.

MARCH 28 (DAY SIXTEEN). This morning the tent's interior
was thick with hoarfrost. We swept it down with our housecleaning
implement of choice — a toilet brush — thus creating a minor
storm. By the end of our first march, the sun was obscured by
dark grey clouds, and a light wind rose from the west. We
stopped to have a cup of coffee, leaning with our backs against a
pressure ridge. It was easy going; Richard seemed to be on the
verge of breaking into a run. But Bob lagged farther and farther
behind. We walked back to him and found him standing with a
dejected look, as if he'd lost something precious to him. "I've
decided to drop the komatik," he said. "I just can't drag it
anymore." We were elated, but tried to disguise our glee. Poor Bob
was heartbroken; the komatik was his boon companion, something he'd loved and cursed, scolded and defended. But now he'd
realized at last that it had to be set aside. Bob is a good travelling
companion, with a lot of experience. He has logged more miles
in the Arctic than either of us. He is strong, good humoured, and
never complains. He would be a great asset to any normal North
Pole expedition. However, this is not a normal trip.

We helped him repack his gear. Bob took the lids from his
Norcaboggans, turning them upside down to make a second pair
of small sleds. The trouble is that all four sleds will be somewhat
less rigid and (worse yet) open to the elements. But anything is
better than the clumsy komatik. Emptied of its load, it looked
like a boat cast up on the shore. Indeed, Bob seemed to be leaving
it like a sacrifice to the Arctic gods. Perhaps we should have made
a Viking funeral pyre or done a ritual dance around its skeleton.
Our optimism rose immediately: barring other factors, our speed
was bound to increase.

CHAPTER SIX

MARCH 31 (DAY NINETEEN). In the evening, we reclined like sleepy bears after a substantial meal. During the day, we'd been in touch by radio with Jean, who relayed a message — or, rather, a query — from Liane: "What are your chances of success?"

This is not what you might term unqualified belief in our abilities, but we can understand the scepticism of observers in the south. To them, the entire venture must appear hopeless. We've been averaging only three miles (6 km) a day; at this rate, it will take us 130 days to reach the Pole, let alone return. But we've reached a turning point. Bob, accustomed now to his new sleds, is keeping pace much better than before. Our loads will lighten with each passing day, as we consume more of our food. The ice will improve, so will the weather, and away we'll go at a great rate. The only thing we lack is sufficient rest. During our first march each day, we look like sleepwalkers, barely able to keep our eyes open, our arms and legs moving feebly and automatically. This evening, Misha fell asleep while dictating his diary, and the tape recorder continued to roll until the end of the mini-cassette, capturing only the sound of his breathing and the occasional snore.

APRIL 1 (DAY TWENTY). Today Bob complains for the first time of real hunger. "I want to eat all the time," he says. "Whatever I do eat seems to be insufficient."

Bob reaps what he has sown. As Misha warned him back in Iqaluit, his unwise choice of personal foods has left him short of calories every day. It's only three to four hundred calories a day (about 5 per cent) less than us, but it seems to be making a big difference. How soon will his clothing prove inadequate as well?

But poor diet is perhaps the most serious shortcoming of all. The early explorer Frederick Cook was among the first to recognize this fact: "A person's mental development is the result of many years of study, but his physical state is the result of his nourishment during the preceding week."

But what can be done? There is no more food to be had — unless of course we call for outside support, which we have no intention of doing. Richard and Misha's lunches are almost exactly the same: double-smoked bacon, granola bars, and various sorts of nuts. We enjoy these high-calorie, high-energy foods while Bob sits wolfing down his tinned sardines. Our only hope is that he will work his way through his least efficient foods now, at the beginning of the journey, saving the more sensible items for later, when the going becomes more arduous.

Today was the coldest so far: $-45°C$ $(-49°F)$. We are keenly aware that we are walking on water; the air is more humid and chills us to the bone. All three of us have frostbitten noses, and Bob has suffered minor frostbite to one of his toes — the first indication that his wardrobe will let him down. The wind stings our faces like a swarm of bees. Tears well up, and eyelashes freeze. We walk like ghosts — forward and back, then forward again. We pull up our neckwarmers to shield our noses, rubbing our stiffened fingers and hands. But no one languishes or complains. We had expected a measure of pain — it comes with the territory. The only course is to ignore and overcome our suffering. Peary said, "A couple of toes is a small price to pay for the Pole," but we trust that we will not be called upon to make a similar sacrifice.

APRIL 3-4 (DAY TWENTY-TWO). The first "artificial" day so far, which requires a brief explanation. From this point on, a "working," as opposed to a calendar, day can be anything we choose. It can be twenty-five or thirty hours long; it can be a night. In April there's almost no difference at this latitude between night and day.

The sun sinks close to the horizon, but does not wholly disappear. Then, two hours later, it rises again; the dusk doesn't have time to gather. We finish our breakfast at suppertime and begin to march in the evening hours.

Misha has turned cartoonist. At breakfast he noticed that a blister had bubbled up on the side of his thermal cup; he'd left it too close to the glowing stove. The swelling resembled a nose, so he added eyes and a mouth, then signed his handiwork. Now he has a twin, which looks so like him that it raises our sagging spirits. Actually, we may have become too dour for our own good. Yesterday Richard remarked that he missed Christopher Holloway and Max Burton, two of our companions during Polar Bridge, who were always able to put the expedition in good humour. Misha replied that this was true, but that even they became glum when the workload was heavy; so we agreed to postpone our merriment until the job was done.

Today our minds were occupied with sober calculations. Did we have enough fuel, food, and time to accomplish our quest? In order, the answers were yes, maybe, and maybe not. Fuel is the least of our worries. It will last, even though we've burned more than we'd anticipated during the past few days of hard frost. Our food supply is rather more problematic. We've estimated that the return trip will take ninety-eight days, plus or minus two or three at most. But we are lagging far behind schedule, and it appears that we will need an extra eight to ten days' travel. If we continue to consume food at the same rate, we will run out well short of Ward Hunt. Thus, we have to reduce our daily ration, without driving ourselves to the brink of exhaustion. Yesterday Richard felt as if he was in debt to his body, burning more calories than he ate. Now is not the time to push ourselves too hard; we have to build our strength in preparation for a final dash, when we'll be called upon to go non-stop, depleting all our physical and mental reserves.

Time itself is the most imponderable question of all. We

started late, and have fallen behind en route. What will we
encounter on our way to the Pole? Even if conditions improve
and our pace accelerates, the earliest that we can hope to arrive
back at Ward Hunt is now the third week of June. When will the
spring breakup begin? Will we be able to reach the island, or will
our path be blocked by the disintegrating ice? That answer to that
question seems far away.

Besides, we have other, more immediate woes and cares. The
final march took all our strength; it seemed to be especially hard
on Bob, although Richard, too, looked more drained than usual.
A different sort of weariness is setting in. Our muscles contract
badly; we lack power and energy, although we feel very little pain.
Perhaps we ought to be content with three marches daily. But
when we stopped, Richard checked our coordinates: 83°51'. We
had covered a mere 2.5 miles (4.6 km)! Also, we found that we
were drifting slightly to the east. The next morning, we checked
again and found that we'd been carried 200 metres (656 ft.) south
and 400 metres (1,312 ft.) to the west. This means that we have
entered an area of more active and random movement, and must
try to get away from it by forging ahead with renewed vigour.

APRIL 4-5 (DAY TWENTY-THREE). Today Bob suddenly
thanked us for our forbearance while he struggled with his
komatik. Richard was pleased by this and hastened to reassure
him. "We're a team," he said, "and when we succeed, our success
will belong to all of us. We'll all be standing on Ward Hunt
together." Misha took advantage of this propitious mood to warn
Bob about his foodstuffs, urging him to make an inventory of
what remained. And Misha was right to worry. Over breakfast
Bob remarked that, when the days began to lengthen, we'd have to
drink more water so as to keep on working. But to get more water,
we'd have to burn more fuel; we couldn't count on melting snow
inside the tent (in a black bag, hung from the ceiling) until mid-

May. This, of course, would throw another wrench into Misha's calculations, and he responded by delivering a mini-lecture to the effect that we had to adapt ourselves to the conditions we faced each day, not vice versa.

That night we heard a hollow rumble deep below us, like an echo of distant thunder. The ice is beginning to break with the coming of spring, and we will soon encounter conditions that will tax us to the fullest.

APRIL 6 (DAY TWENTY-FOUR). A series of marches amid soft snow — hard, laborious, monotonous work. The snow has become our evil genius; our skis leave deep ruts as we go along. Even a blizzard would be welcome now, because it would solidify the topmost crust. In a few days, though, we'll shift over to one-way marches. We must be patient and husband our energies. Meanwhile, Bob continues to cause concern. He sits by himself during our rest breaks, well away from us — but we have seen him eating entire handfuls of raisins; he refuses to ration his supplies as Misha has suggested.

APRIL 8 (DAY TWENTY-SIX). We continue to fight the heavy, clinging snow. We schedule an additional rest period, but it brings no relief. We sleep, eat, and sleep again, losing time with every hour's idleness. If only the Arctic would return to normal! We repeat the same thought over in our minds: let the snow become harder, more rigid, so that we can press on. But the weather does not change. Today, almost as if making a joke, Bob muttered, "I am tired of suffering and struggle." Misha's opinion is that Bob is close to the edge — capable only of reaching the Pole, after which he will collapse and require evacuation.

APRIL 9 (DAY TWENTY-SEVEN). Bob is weaker today. Crossing a pressure ridge, his arms and legs refused to obey him; he moved as if drunk. We fear that a crisis may soon be upon us. Bob has never been in the ice fields before without dogsleds to pull his load. Perhaps the task is beyond his power. And what about his food? The thought that he will exhaust his supplies, forcing us to share with him, is constantly in our minds. Today Misha was crawling over a large drift while Richard struggled below. Misha turned back and shouted, "I will go on to the end! Even if Bob decides to return, there's no other way for me!" Richard came closer and called back, "Don't worry, Misha, I will follow you. If I can't walk anymore, then drag me along – but don't leave me behind."

During the final march, we saw that Bob was lagging half an hour behind. We pressed on, but left a piece of chocolate in the snow, hoping that it would cheer him up. Later, in camp, he thanked Misha and said, "You are a good man." Misha clapped him on the shoulder and said, "No problem." But the problems continue to mount. Bob has become absolutely indifferent to his appearance. It's hard to keep oneself looking half-human in the Arctic at the best of times, but a total disregard for personal hygiene is the first sign of psychological surrender. Increasingly, Bob resembles a man who stands on the brink of a precipice, ready to fall at any moment into terrifying uncertainty. The only good news is that the snow underfoot has changed, becoming a trifle more dense and easier to glide across on our skis. We've done good work today – but Bob confessed that he felt worn out at the end of the first march.

APRIL 10 (DAY TWENTY-EIGHT). A day off, during which Misha determined to force the issue. He insisted that Bob conduct an inventory of his provisions. His personal lunch foods totalled only twenty-six kilograms (57 lb.) – at most, 350 grams (12 oz.) per day for the seventy-three days that remained. Worse yet, they were the worst possible mix – the sardines, some tinned meat, and a

Bob Mantell and John Mordhorst finishing a training session in Iqaluit, February 1992.

Misha crossing one of the innumerable cracks that slowed our progress to a crawl of five miles (9 km) a day.

Only Misha's quick reaction prevents him from falling into the water while crossing thin ice disguised with a layer of snow. Note the ski tracks and the hole.

Driftwood locked in the Arctic Ocean. It probably originated somewhere in Russia, drifting down a river and into the open sea.

Skiing on the Arctic Ocean, in good weather . . .

. . . and in the bad weather and broken ice that finally convinced us to give up in June 1992.

Josée Auclair, Richard's wife, did most of our custom sewing.

Liane Benoit, 1992 expedition manager.

Bob Mantell

Our expedition tent with radio antenna set up using skis and poles. The tent has no frame, only a ski as a centre pole.

Richard communicating by radio while on the trail. It was often a very cold, but unavoidable, job (the problem with a pre-set radio schedule).

Bob, hauling his big wooden sled.

An example of the pressure ridges that made it difficult for Bob to follow our old trail back to Ward Hunt Island. The trail, heaved up by the ice, is still just visible here. Bob's pack and sled are in the foreground. (Photo: Bob Mantell)

Relatively easy conditions. If only more days could have been like this.

Richard and Misha at the pickup by a First Air Twin Otter, June 22, 1992.

piece of smoked salmon. Misha asked Bob to think about how long these supplies would last, at what rate he would consume them. But Bob flared up. "Why are you treating me like a child?" he said. "I can manage for myself." Our point exactly – he could not do so, and all of us would suffer if he continued in his ways.

APRIL 11 (DAY TWENTY-NINE). Peary was right: "It is impossible to forecast or to calculate the appearance of open leads. On your way to the North they hinder your progress; on the way back they cut off travellers from the continent and from life." In 1906, Peary was stopped in his tracks by a vast body of open water he called the Big Lead, which proved impossible to cross. Today, during our second march, we hit a similar expanse, as opposed to smaller, more easily bridgeable cracks. The lead was twenty metres (66 ft.) wide, covered with thin, mouse-grey ice. In some places, there was no ice at all – only black water, emitting smoke-like fumes. The wind blew from the northeast. At the place where the lead turned to the wind at right angles, the ice was breaking up at the edges. Small pieces crawled over one another, moving like living things, with crashing, gritting sounds. We had to move quickly, too – the lead might open wider at any moment. We walked along it and found a place only a half-metre (2 ft.) wide where we could safely cross, taking with us the first part of our load. We sat down on the opposite side and had a snack before returning for the rest of our supplies. As we did so, the lead closed before our eyes. The ice floes arched their backs to the sky, giving birth to new pressure ridges. We took off our backpacks and began to play tag among the newborn hummocks like children in a playground. Only Bob hung back; he did not share our enthusiasm for foolish games.

APRIL 12 (DAY THIRTY). Bright sun and dead calm; our voices cut the silence like knives. We thought again of Will Steger, who one day was standing alone on the ice, troubled by a dull and rhythmic pounding. He looked around, but the other members of his expedition were nowhere near; nor did the ice surface seem to be in motion. Suddenly, he realized that he was listening to the beating of his heart.

We sweated heavily during our first march and were at once transformed into walking ice sculptures, encrusted with hoarfrost from head to foot. But during lunch, our upbeat mood evaporated. Bob had stealthily taken a quantity of nuts from his food supply and gobbled them down as if there were no tomorrow. Misha flew into a sudden temper, Bob protested that he could make the nuts last for as long as might be necessary, and Misha tried again to make him realize that the nuts should be conserved for later use, when he would need them more. But once again, we feared that this advice fell on deaf ears.

As we began our third march, Misha saw — or thought he saw — a number of strange, dark objects in the distance. Hallucination or reality? We skied nearer and discovered that they were a backpack, a pair of skis, and ski poles standing upright in the snow. Then a ski trace and the marks of dogsleds could be clearly discerned — the path of Martin Williams and the Norwegians. The backpack was filled with frozen socks, underwear, and boots; some poor soul had fallen in the water. We rummaged through it more thoroughly and found a granola bar, which we ate for dessert that night. The ski trace appears to be between two and five weeks old. In some places it is covered in snow, but it stretches conveniently northward, following almost exactly the same path we plan to take. It will be easier to follow it, rather than break our own trail in the virgin snow — our first real stroke of luck.

APRIL 13 (DAY THIRTY-ONE). We followed the Norwegians' path all morning long, although with some misgivings. We debated seriously whether making use of their trail would constitute "support." We decided that it wouldn't, and Richard cited histor-ical precedent. If Robert Peary had stumbled on Frederick Cook's trail, he said, Peary would have followed it like a shot. We'd come across the present-day trail by pure accident; we hadn't asked for a favour. Besides (because the Norwegians were travelling with dogs), the trail was somewhat more twisting and roundabout than the route we'd otherwise have taken, so we gained some, lost some, on the deal.

Soon we entered a large area of badly broken ice. Two weeks ago, Jean had told us that the Norwegians were slogging through a very rough patch; obviously this was it. Three seventy-five-minute marches took us forward only 3.5 miles (6.5 km). We had to shuttle back and forth repeatedly; our return trips added up to more than an hour and a half. How bored we are with this tedious to and fro! How eagerly we look forward to the day when we can carry our load in one direction only – to the north.

Bob sat apart from us again while eating his lunch. Our food is in clear plastic bags, but he hoards his foodstuffs in a solid nylon bag; only he can see what he is taking from it. We fear that he is continuing to misuse his dwindling supplies.

This evening he huddled in a corner of the tent, eating some-thing – we couldn't see what. But we could actually smell the odour of the nuts! He forgets that, although our tastebuds may be dulled, our sense of smell is strangely heightened. Misha exploded once more. "Stop eating those!" he shouted. "Leave them till a better time – or a worse, when you'll really need them. I swear that, when we reach the Pole, I'm going to check your supplies, item by item."

"Don't worry," Bob replied. "Everything will be all right." This is his usual response to any criticism; he seems weirdly composed; secure in his opinions. But daily he offers new cause for concern. He has acquired an old man's walk; he coughs slightly and his appearance continues to deteriorate. During our third shuttle march, we were walking back up along our own trail, which was well-trodden and impossible to miss, yet Bob veered seriously off course. One morning he actually started off from camp in the wrong direction. All these things only fill us with apprehension.

At least the fact that we can still follow the Norwegians' two-week-old ski trace proves that the ice has not begun to drift to any great degree. Peary was on the ice at almost this same time; perhaps he could, as he claimed, have followed his own trail back to the south, moving from igloo to igloo. This adds credence to his claim that he skied from wherever he got to (that point, at least, remains in grave dispute) back to Cape Columbia in an extraordinary seventeen days.

APRIL 14-15 (DAY THIRTY-TWO). Today we made camp at 84°20', having set a record for a single day's marches – four miles (7 km) north. To our surprise, Bob is moving well – more strongly than he did at the beginning of the journey.

As for Richard, he seemed to run at full speed along the ski trace. Misha attempted to match his pace but failed. He reflected gloomily that Richard was both five years younger and the more proficient skier. Richard has begun to use a zinc-oxide ointment for protection against the sun and wind. The effect is primitive and strange; he looks like the ancient Britons, who painted their faces with woad before going into battle.

APRIL 16-17 (DAY THIRTY-FOUR). We've decided to rest, having moved another four miles (7 km) closer to the Pole. We debated the length of the rest period and settled on two full days. As usual, Bob did not involve himself in our conversation. He seemed deeply absorbed in his own thoughts. He still kept pace with us much better than before, although his silence and indifference fell like a curtain between us. He continued to gorge himself in secret. Once, Richard found the wrapper of a granola bar, half buried in the snow. According to plan, Bob should have kept his stock of these bars in reserve, eating them only during the expedition's final forty or fifty days.

APRIL 18 (DAY THIRTY-FIVE). Richard led the way during our first march, but then Bob took the lead, walking so quickly and powerfully that we could scarcely keep up with him. Just as we'd stopped for a rest and were taking off our backpacks, he said, "Guys, I need to talk about my leaving the expedition."

We stiffened like two figures in a waxworks; for a moment, we couldn't grasp what he was saying.

"I want to turn back," he continued. "I'm going to make my own way to Ward Hunt."

Misha was the first to recover his wits. "Well, Bob," he said, "that's not such a bad idea. If you can't go forward, you must of course return. If you succeed in reaching Ward Hunt, you'll prove your strength beyond all doubt. To ski solo from this latitude would be a remarkable achievement. And, to be selfish, by not calling for an airlift out, you'll maintain the expedition's unsupported status."

We could go no farther that day; we had to absorb the many implications of Bob's decision. We pitched the tent and began to eat tremendous quantities of food. We can afford to do so; now there is no question of Bob's running short and our having to share our supplies with him.

After our meal, Bob tried to explain himself further. "This expedition is not for me," he said. "I feel as if I'm off on an island of my own — I'm not part of the team. You're different — you do your jobs, perform the same amount of work as I've done, and still you can calculate the miles, discuss all sorts of things. I love the Arctic, but all I'm doing is staring down at the trail. I could pass right by a polar bear and not even see it. The whole thing's too hard; I've bitten off more than I can chew."

Misha was doubtful; he wanted to be sure that Bob's decision was founded on practical considerations, not on a moment of passing weakness.

"Are you quite sure you want to do this?" he asked. "You're in good shape; we don't doubt that your physical state will enable you to continue."

Bob cut him off. "I've made up my mind," he said. "All the fun, all the motivation, is gone. My clothes, my foodstuffs, are all much worse than yours. That's my own fault. But there are things you don't know. I've eaten all my chocolate — all nineteen bars."

We laughed aloud; we'd never even guessed. We knew how we treasured and gloated over our own tiny shards of chocolate; they were our special rewards. And all the time, while we were busy in the mornings, repacking our gear and fretting over our dwindling supplies, Bob had been off behind a snowdrift, consuming his entire ration.

And so a new plan was formulated. Bob would leave, retracing his steps to Ward Hunt. He'd take with him enough supplies to last for at least twelve days — two weeks, if he managed to restrain his appetite. That should be more than sufficient; he'd be marching and skiing alone, burdened only with his backpack and one small sled. The three of us had taken five weeks to come this far, fully loaded every step of the way.

He would also take one of our TUBSAT transmitter/receivers* so that he could call for help at any point. We asked him again

---

* TUBSAT stands for Technical University of Berlin Satellite, which is what the hand-held unit communicates with, either transmitting or receiving short messages. At the time, there were very few of these devices in use anywhere in the world. We had two, as did another expedition in Antarctica. Of course, the university could download a message at any time or transmit one of its own.

For a full description of the TUBSAT system as it was used on our 1995 expedition, see the note on page 99.

whether he wished to summon a plane; this would have been by far the safer course, but he insisted that he would walk. He said that he wanted a chance to be by himself and think things over — and that when he got to Ward Hunt, he hoped he'd be able to sit for a couple of days before the plane arrived. That evening, as we were about to fall asleep, we realized that Bob had decided to turn back several days before, which accounted for his newfound strength in the final marches. He'd straightened his shoulders and become calm and confident. He was his former self, the Bob we'd known when we recruited him. But, having made his decision, he was torn by conflicting emotions. He wished to retreat, but was forced to press on. No wonder he'd struggled and behaved in what seemed to us an irrational manner. But now he is clear in his mind, and we know that he will make it safely back to Ward Hunt. He is a good person, whole-hearted and decent. No blame attaches to his failure; few people would even dream of undertaking such a trial. We are thankful for his generous and reasonable decision, which demanded great inner courage. We hope that we will perform as well, now that the burden is ours alone to bear.

CHAPTER SEVEN

APRIL 22 (DAY THIRTY-NINE). Today we parted from Bob, a difficult moment after so many ordeals. We embraced, and he set off for the south. His figure receded in the distance and was lost from sight. We were saddened, but could not afford to dwell on things that might have been. Our challenge lies ahead; we must look towards what will be.

Our loads have suddenly become heavier, because we redivided the food and shared equipment. We will take with us rations for seventy-three travelling days. Some of the gear is abandoned where we stand, but each of us is now responsible for 160 kilograms (353 lb.) — two 60-kilogram (132-lb.) sleds and a single backpack. From this point on, we will try to take the entire load at once; our shuttle marches are a thing of the past. When the surface is flat, we can maintain a normal speed, but any obstacle slows us more than before. We enter an area of severely broken and fragmented ice; six marches bring us only two miles (4 km) closer to the Pole.

APRIL 23 (DAY FORTY). This morning we shifted our loads around, trying to achieve a better balance between backpacks and sleds. We continued to follow the Norwegians' ski trail until noon, when the sun grew dim and leaden clouds congested the sky. The ice surface lost all semblance of shading and shadow; the milk-white haze enveloped us, and anything beyond arm's length disappeared from view. When we first set off from Ward Hunt, we'd had to concentrate intently on searching out a route through the hummocks and pressure ridges. Now, however, we proceeded almost automatically, as if by intuition.

By the end of the fourth march, we encountered a fresh lead, the result of the wind that had raged around our tent all during the previous night. We were unable to find a crossing place and had to walk almost two kilometres (1 mi.) along its length before finding a surface that, although riddled with small cracks, enabled us to go forward. By doing so, we left the Norwegians' ski track, and would never sight it again. Richard sighed and said, with literal truth, "We are side-stepping to the Pole." On we went, for two more marches, through soft snow and wind-pressed crests. We could not see, and feared that we were making almost no progress at all. But in the evening, we found that we'd managed to cover 3.2 more miles (5.9 km).

We made camp, and our thoughts turned to Bob's lonely march. Would he be able to follow our previous trail, or had it been obliterated by the storm? If so, he might camp and wait for the weather to improve – but this would add time to his journey and deplete his food supply.

The evening before we parted, we'd taken out the videocamera and asked him to state, for the record, why he was turning back. He talked about "personal misconceptions" and "reaching his personal limits." He stressed, during a radio contact, that his physical health presented no problem; it wasn't a medical situation. But he added that he felt "some deterioration of mental health." When we asked him to talk about the reason for his departure, we were thinking only about the documentary film we hoped would result from the expedition, but now we were relieved that we had taken what might prove to be a precautionary step. During another radio contact, we learned that the RCMP – who'd been informed that Bob was returning solo – were expressing a fair degree of curiosity about the state of our relations at the moment we parted.

It dawned on us that lurid rumours were almost certainly spreading in the distant south. What were the police insinuating? Perhaps the authorities – who after all would have to search for Bob if he failed to arrive at Ward Hunt on schedule – suspected that there'd been bad blood between us and that we'd driven him away. Who knew what sorts of far-fetched murder-mystery plots were being debated back in the world outside?

We were convinced that no harm could befall him. He carried a radio as well as a TUBSAT unit. Even if this equipment were to fail or get lost, he had a compass and sextant and knew how to use them. The weather might delay him, but he would be perfectly all right – perhaps in better shape than we were, because he was going home.

APRIL 25 (DAY FORTY-TWO). The previous evening, we'd made
a side bet with the Arctic: If there was sun the next morning,
we'd have an extra cup of coffee with our breakfast porridge. But
no such luck. We turned on the GPS and found that we had
drifted 700 metres (2,300 ft.) northward during the night. This
was not unalloyed good news; it meant that we would soon be
facing open water again. And so we were, almost immediately.
We saw a new lead in the distance, covered with fresh, young ice.
As far as we could see, the air was filled with dense, violet-
coloured fog.

We scouted to and fro, making slow progress across the lead's
tributaries or channel branches. The wind threw damp, sticky
snow into our faces. Later in the day, the sun appeared, but
brought with it a new difficulty. Misha felt as if his eyes were
filled with sand – the first symptoms of snow blindness. One's
eyes tire quickly in the Arctic sunlight as it reflects off an infinity
of white. We put on our sunglasses, whose tinted lenses immediately transformed the world around us to crimson and purple.

APRIL 26 (DAY FORTY-THREE). Only 30 per cent of the way to
the Pole. The hardest day thus far – the sort of day Misha refers
to as Big Punishment. After two marches, Richard felt as if he'd
done at least twice that number. Nothing could extricate his sled
from the snow; it gripped the runners like a parking brake. The
sleds wouldn't glide; they had to be dragged, even on a downhill
slope. Misha made better going, by dint of sheer brute strength –
but even he was leaning on his ski poles for support. On days like
this, Misha compares us to circus animals. We perform amazing
tricks and are rewarded with food. But the food is never enough
to satisfy us or make us drowsy. Instead, it keeps us going,
jumping through the next frigid hoop, until the next break, the
next insubstantial reward.

APRIL 28 (DAY FORTY-FIVE). The drift continues to drag us back by day and night. Spring is coming in the southern latitudes, but we slog on, across mammoth ice floes cut with a myriad cracks. All day we wander in the labyrinth of ice hummocks, looming grey and formless in the hanging fog. Suddenly we bump against an unusual, darkish spot. A layer of soil was lying atop the ice! It was small – perhaps thirty centimetres (12 in.) wide by a metre (3 ft.) long – a touch of home that made Misha think about the ice of the Taimyr Peninsula, far away on the Russian side of the Pole. This ice floe had been brought by the current from some other sea; how many weeks or years had it taken to complete its long journey? (Some ice floes are very dirty indeed; we took a photograph of Misha skiing in what almost looks like mud.) We inspected the floe and saw that strands of seaweed had been frozen into its surface. They ranged in colour from green through brown to rusty red; they looked quite fresh, as if in suspended animation. They reminded us of Feodor Konyukhov, a Polar Bridge member and an artist by profession, who in 1991 had made a solo journey to the Pole. During it he'd almost starved. In the extremity of his hunger, he'd come across just this sort of ice floe, chopped off a piece, and enjoyed an unexpected delicacy. We are not quite that ravenous yet, but Richard looked at the seaweed and shouted out, "Fe-o-dor! Here is your favourite – edible ice!"

It is now eight days since we parted from Bob. In four more, if he stays on course and makes good time, he should come to Ward Hunt.

We are concerned about our fuel supply; perhaps Bob was right to have brought more. We have been burning 600 grams (21 oz.) daily, but now that we are behind schedule, we will have to ration it with care. We can probably do without our mid-morning and afternoon tea, and make do with warm, not boiling, water for breakfast coffee. And there can be no more heating of the tent. We use a cover over the pot and stove that conserves heat and fuel, but leaves the tent like a freezer.

APRIL 29 (DAY FORTY-SIX). Today we received a radio message from Jean, stating that a search would begin for Bob twelve days after the day we separated. But this is nonsensical – he will be able to prolong his food supplies for at least a week more than his anticipated twelve days' time. Why are the authorities in such a rush? Why do they wish to fabricate a crisis when none exists? Most search-and-rescue operations are mounted simply to retrieve local people who wander off while hunting; perhaps the prospect of tracking down a missing polar explorer is too much to resist.

For several days now, we've been discussing whether we can afford to take a two-hour rest after our fourth march. We tried this today, to see whether it would restore our strength. It did – but we were in need of all the strength we could summon up. The ice has changed, and we are again in the midst of soft snow and never-ending pressure ridges.

This evening we found that we'd made another 5.7 miles (10.5 km) – our record thus far. It's hard to believe that we managed to walk eight marches of fifty minutes each, carrying 145 kilograms (320 lb.) per man. So we will try to take an afternoon rest each day, at least until the load lightens further or the weather improves.

APRIL 30 (DAY FORTY-SEVEN). Another record – the warmest day en route. Although there's no sun, the temperature is −8.5°C (17°F). We feel as if we are walking inside a giant greenhouse. At least the sleds are moving better than ever. As every skier knows, you glide along by putting pressure on the snow crust, thus creating friction, which melts the molecules of the topmost layer. You're actually travelling on water – except when the temperature falls below −20°C (−4°F), the crust doesn't melt, and you slide on ice crystals instead. The colder it gets, the less well anything — be it a ski or a sled runner — slides. But during the evening, the temperature dropped again, and we were back to normal, feeling as if we were dragging the sleds through sand.

MAY 1-2 (DAY FORTY-EIGHT). Bob's food supplies will run out today, unless he's had the will to cut back his rations. He hasn't yet attempted to communicate with the outside world, but we remain convinced that this is due to some sort of technical failure. In other words, his batteries may be dead, but he is alive and well.

MAY 4 (DAY FIFTY). Yesterday evening we walked another 7.3 miles (13.5 km) closer to the Pole. Now we have decided to rest for forty-eight hours, because we have taxed ourselves to the limit. During one rest period, we tried to nap, but kept fading in and out of consciousness. Misha felt as if his head had become detached from his body. He tried to but could not arise; his limbs seemed filled with lead. We slept for almost five hours, before continuing our work.

Our location is now 85°19'. We have covered fifty miles (93 km) in twelve days, an outstanding achievement. But what has become of Bob? No one has heard a word from him, and he is probably out of food.

The rest of the news, via our radio, is no better. Jean told Richard that the general opinion in Resolute is that we will fail in our attempt. Josée is going through a very difficult time; she has become depressed about Richard's absence and fears that he is pushing himself too hard. How difficult it is for him to receive such messages when there is nothing he can say to reassure her.

MAY 5 (DAY FIFTY-ONE). Tomorrow we must move on, more rested than we've been for weeks. Meanwhile, Jean reports that

Martin Williams and the Norwegians, having reached the Pole, had been flown to Resolute. On the way up, this flight checked into Ward Hunt, but Bob had not arrived. The pilots then flew north along our route. We didn't see or hear them overhead, but they identified the spot where we'd parted from Bob and glimpsed his abandoned komatik. Tomorrow a full-scale search-and-rescue operation will begin, using infrared heat-sensing devices. We have our doubts about the efficiency of infrared technology; it's not nearly as effective as its proponents would have everyone believe. The planes are hard-pressed to find a whole herd of muskox, let alone a single person, fully dressed and bending every effort not to release any heat when he camps for the night. But Bob's disappearance (real or imagined) is causing great concern in the south and has garnered a great deal of attention from the media.

What has become of our friend? Now we imagine any number of dire possibilities. He could have been attacked by a bear. The pilots had reported that many large leads cut across our trail; he might have fallen into open water and drowned. But not necessarily. In fact, it seemed more likely that he's been forced to detour around them, sending him off course in one direction or another. We cling to the belief that he still considers himself to be a member of our unsupported expedition and is striving to make it back under his own steam. But a message via TUBSAT warns us that there are indeed bears in our vicinity. The two of us would make a more substantial meal than Bob alone. We check our gun — a .357 magnum revolver, which we hope will be as effective against bears as it is against the villains in Clint Eastwood's films — and keep a sharp lookout all day long.

Soon new messages come thick and fast. The pilots have located Bob's tent, less than twenty miles (37 km) north of Ward Hunt, but he is nowhere in sight. The plane's fuel was low, and they could not continue to search. They'd seen three bears not far from the spot that Bob turned back, but the animals were heading due north, hot on our trail. Perhaps bears know how to count heads, or sniff out larger quantities of food. Richard added another cartridge to the revolver.

MAY 6-7 (DAY FIFTY-TWO). Hooray! Bob has been found at 83°20', fifteen miles (28 km) from Ward Hunt; he'd had it in sight for two days. He was safe and sound and somewhat surprised at all the fuss surrounding his alleged disappearance. Apparently, he'd managed to follow our trail for forty-eight hours, but encountered the white haze and lost sight of our previous route throughout the rest of his trek. He walked by means of his compass and was saving the TUBSAT for emergencies. He'd also managed to ration his supplies, because he was moving slowly. He was in good spirits at all times and never in any real danger. So all the searches were premature – a panic reaction in the world outside. As well, Richard is happy to learn that Josée is in better spirits. Buoyed by all this good news, we set another record today – 7.45 miles (13.8 km) closer to our goal.

MAY 8-9 (DAY FIFTY-FOUR). We'd estimated that the maximum length of the expedition, allowing for every conceivable delay, would be 110 days, so here we are, at the halfway point – an important psychological boost. Our spirits are up, and we decide to dispense with our afternoon naps, unless we run into more soft, clinging snow. If the ice is normal, we propose to march all day with only minimal stops.

MAY 9-10 (DAY FIFTY-FIVE). A wide strip of open water barred our path, and we were forced to walk along it for most of the day. Finally, we noticed yet another lead, covered with what we at first thought was young ice, but proved to be more like barely congealed brine, intermingled with gritty salt crystals. We felt as if our skis were Velcroed to the surface. Worse yet, the lead began to close as we neared the other side, buckling the ice we stood on. We struggled across and camped on the opposite bank. In the morning, not a sign of the lead remained – only fresh pressure ridges where hours before there had been open water.

MAY 10-11 (DAY FIFTY-SIX). A very strange and disheartening message arrives via TUBSAT. Vowels reinserted, it reads: "Pilots refuse Pole landing after May 28. Recommend reduction to three weeks supply and polar dash. Need answer by May 13. Bob is OK. Expect solar flares. Liane."

Translated, this means that our advisers want us to abort the mission – or at least to contravene its founding principle. They are urging us to throw away everything except enough food to last us for twenty-one days and make a run for the Pole. Having reached it, we can abandon our gear (and all hope of returning unsupported to Ward Hunt), stand around grinning for the cameras, climb aboard a plane, and go home. First Air's pilots have unilaterally decided that conditions at or near the Pole will prohibit them from picking us up any later than the end of the month. Exactly how they reached this decision remains obscure – they aren't here, and we are. We know that they'd have difficulty touching down in wet snow, but who can be sure whether that's what they'll encounter? It's nice to know that Bob is okay, but we knew that already. As for solar flares, we don't much care, although they may affect our radio transmissions.

The message deserved a response, and we transmitted one: "Greetings to all. We are in excellent shape. Pole June 9. Ward Hunt in early July. Continue discussions with pilots."

The Pole itself is nothing; we've been there twice already. Getting there and back, as specified, is the order of the day – so we'd better get moving. We continue to trust in our own abilities, our own assessments of the situation.

Today Misha turned his hand to graphic arts, writing a

message on the rear of his sled. It reads: "Smile, Richard!" Everyone knows what the sled dog sees when it follows the leader — but even humans tend to fix their gaze on the sled in front as it bounces along the trail. Later, when it was his turn to lead, Richard responded by decking his sled with a reply, in Russian, reading: "Be happy, Misha!"

Well, if that were impossible, at least we could be satisfied that we are doing our utmost. Jack London wrote that "when two men go together along the white silence, it is not important that one works more, and the other, less. The thing that matters is that each of them should do everything in his power." On that score, at least, we have no reason to reproach ourselves.

CHAPTER EIGHT

MAY 12 (DAY FIFTY-SEVEN). A quiet morning, with coffee — everyday Arctic life. We live amid this cold white sea so naturally that one would think we'd never known another, more cosseted existence. We prolong our pleasure, taking small, careful sips, and discuss our plans for the day. We are in good shape and moving reasonably well. We can count on making seven miles (13 km) a day, in seven to nine marches. We could strive to cover more distance, but it's sensible to pace ourselves. Yesterday we made eight marches under very difficult conditions, and nine marches the day before. We must be careful not to rush heedlessly ahead. The Arctic will detect and take advantage of our weariness — just as we can almost sense its aversion to our every footstep.

After covering only a very short distance, our path was blocked by a range of pressure ridges. We took off our packs, unhitched the sleds, and began to reconnoitre to and fro. Just as we'd identified a likely pathway, Misha fell into the water. Or, to be precise, his right leg went down beneath the surface, drenching him to the knee. Everything around us had looked so simple and straightforward – a textbook example, Arctic 101. Indeed, it was a textbook pitfall for the inattentive. Two ice floes had collided, the pressure ridges had thrust up, and the ice beneath them had sunk down and been covered with water, which in turn was covered by drifting snow. So there sat Misha, working his way through complex and colourful Russian curses while wringing out his socks.

Next we advanced with great difficulty for little more than a quarter-mile (0.5 km), and came upon a place that seemed to have sprung not from the pages of a textbook but from darkest nightmare. Immediately in front of us, cutting across our path at right angles, was something that neither of us had seen before – something we couldn't have predicted would exist.

We knew that we were in a friction zone, atop the edge of the Lomonosov Ridge, an underwater mountain range that intersects with the Greenland current. Instead of simply drifting apart, thus producing leads, ice floes here rub back and forth against each other, producing bands of chewed-up ice. A typical lead is bad enough, but it's really nothing more than a large crack filled with water. If it's wide enough, it may have waves, but the water doesn't usually flow; there's no current. Nor are the banks or sides moving to any great degree. What we were looking at wasn't a lead – it was a river of ice that flowed past us at a slow walking pace. There was virtually no open water – just a tightly packed mush. Sometimes there were ice whirlpools; the floating blocks and shards of ice would churn and somersault chaotically around like clothes in a washing machine. Everything was moving simultaneously, but at different speeds in different areas. We climbed the nearest pressure ridge, but no end could be seen. Nor could we see the river's opposite bank. From time to time, a portion of the seething mass would seem to stop, as if trying to latch onto the bank on which we stood. All movement would subside, almost cease. But then the great jumble of ice would start its tearing, churning motion once more.

Despite its menacing appearance, the ice river made very little sound – only a dismal rustle and muffled splashes that made it seem even creepier and more malevolent. There was nowhere to turn, so we decided to await developments, and sat there drinking tea. Perhaps the river itself decided to take a break; one of its sections slowed to a virtual halt. We couldn't stay where we were indefinitely, so we ventured onto its surface in search of a reasonably large and stable floe. To do this, we had to step first onto a stretch of compressed slush, probing ahead of us with the tips of our ski poles. Unfortunately, by doing this, we violated the most basic rule of Arctic travel – never, under any circumstances, abandon your gear. We were so bemused by the sight of the ice river that we'd wandered onto it without our backpacks. Now they – and our sleds – were floating away from us. Or, to be more exact, we were floating away from them. The surface we were balancing on threatened to become a crazy whirlpool again. Our supplies were at least twenty metres (66 ft.) distant, growing farther away with each passing second. We tore off our skis and stepped gingerly from one small piece of ice to another, until we reached a spot where we could bend down, replace our skis, and slide back across the frozen slush to the safety of the bank.

Now we were reunited with our gear, and several more hours passed. The river's movement ebbed and flowed, but we did not feel confident enough to test its surface again. Finally, we saw a huge, flat pan – the size of several football fields – coming slowly down the river. We couldn't see its far side, so we hoped that the pan might be the river's opposite bank. We waited until its passing had compressed and stiffened the slush, then managed to cross a smaller floe perhaps twenty square metres (215 sq. ft.) that

lay between us and the giant pan. This time we took care to strap
on our backpacks and pull our sleds behind us. But no sooner had
we reached the smaller floe than the current swept it away from
the pan we'd hoped to reach. About six metres (20 ft.) of churning water lay between, and it could not be bridged. For yet
another hour we were forced to stay put, balancing on the small
floe and separated from the pan by about the width of a city
street. We couldn't retreat, even if we'd wanted to; the bank we'd
abandoned was out of reach as well. In other words, we'd become
part of the moving river.

Eventually, the end of the giant pan came into sight. It was
about to pass us by, moving more quickly than our floe. It was
followed by another stretch of crushed and broken ice – and then,
at a greater distance, by a mammoth, floating pressure ridge that
had somehow broken free of the pack ice. Now it came sailing
down the river, travelling at deceptive speed. Its leading edge
looked exactly like the sharp prow of an ice-breaker. At first it
seemed to be moving slowly, but we had been deceived by its bulk.
In fact, it was bearing down on us with terrifying rapidity.

In a matter of minutes, it was almost on top of us. We had
nowhere to run. It collided with the edge of our small ice floe,
which promptly split in two. The portion on which we were so
precariously balanced began to tilt at a crazy angle. It was being
overridden by the crushing weight of the pressure ridge; driven
down into the frigid water. We struggled to keep our footing, but
we knew that we were about to slide off into the ocean.

"We have no chance to get out of here," Richard said.

Then Misha, for some reason he'll never know, turned towards
the monster that threatened to drive us down and said three times
– in English! – "It must stop."

It didn't, but it seemed to slow and began to push us along in
front of it, rather like a train engine shunting a railway car. It
nudged us closer to the pan that we'd been trying to reach.

Suddenly, everything — our small floe, the large pan, and the looming pressure ridge — was moving at exactly the same speed. The end of the pan lay very close to us, across a narrow band of icy slush. This, too, was being squeezed and solidified by the pressure ridge, but, at any second, everything might revert to whirling motion again.

At that moment, Misha stepped off our ice floe and into the Arctic Ocean — or, more precisely, onto the momentarily solid slush. The edge of the pan was higher than the surface of the slush by half a metre (2 ft.); he'd have to jump up onto it, if he could succeed in getting across. But in he stepped, carrying his backpack and pulling both his sleds. It was madness — but it was our only hope, and Richard was quick to follow. The ice began to shudder all around us; the slushy surface, disturbed by Misha's passing, began to disintegrate beneath Richard's feet. Misha held out his hand and helped Richard drag his sleds onto the bobbing pan. We looked back and saw the small floe that we'd just abandoned go down into the whirlpool. Only its tip was visible, like a ship that rears its prow to the sky before sinking beneath the waves.

The things that seem to us so matter-of-fact — skiing across barely frozen slush with nothing below it but hundreds of metres of water, or moving like tightrope walkers across a bridge of skis — may sound to many people like death-defying stunts. Actually, to the experienced Arctic traveller, they're almost second nature — standard procedure ever since Robert Peary's day. As a result, the Arctic traveller is very seldom afraid. Every moment of every day, we are aware of the need for caution. Often we are exhausted to the point of collapse, in some degree of discomfort if not actual pain. Fear for one's life is something else again. But when we saw how the floating pressure ridge consumed our small ice floe, munching it up as we would a tasty dessert, both of us were afraid. We embraced — too modest a celebration of the fact that we were, against all odds, alive. We decided that, when we made it safely home, we would both appoint the 12th of May as our second birthday.

But we had no chance or cause for further celebration. We'd gained the ice pan, but were still in motion, part of the awful river. Plainly, the pan was not the river's opposite bank, so we had to look for a way to escape from it. The ice was cracking very close to us, and we concluded that the pan was being chipped away by the impact of other floes. We began to explore its far edge, but in vain. We'd been on our feet for twelve hours straight, and we had to rest, no matter how great the danger. The centre of the pan looked solid enough to make camp; besides, we had no alternative. So Misha suggested that we adopt the only course of action that seemed remotely productive under the circumstances: "Consult our pillows." We agreed that we would set our alarm clock and take turns checking on the situation every two hours throughout the night. It seemed unlikely that we would sleep for longer than that at a time, if at all.

Misha slept badly, his dreams fraught with visions of some dreadful abyss that yawned and beckoned him closer. In his half-awake state, the sound of the ice in motion was oddly muted, like a person groaning quietly in an adjacent room. Then it seemed as if ghosts, or at least some sort of undefined, immaterial beings, were luring him onward to his doom. Perhaps, he thought, they were the unquiet souls of Arctic travellers who'd met their fates amid the shifting ice. But he fought against these oppressive visions. With every step forward, he convinced himself, we evidenced our superiority over the blind, inanimate forces of nature. Despite them, we were alive and could not turn back now.

MAY 13 (DAY FIFTY-EIGHT). Richard was the first to be roused by the alarm. Stepping outside the tent, he saw at once that our pan was still an island in the middle of the river, and still intact, even though it, too, was diminishing in size. When it crashed against the other floes, either a fragment would break off or a pressure ridge would begin to build. These fresh ridges were crawling closer and closer to our tent. He awoke Misha, who began his turn at watch. Richard then fell asleep – and did not awaken in time to relieve Misha, but no harm was done, because the situation appeared to have stabilized.

Actually, it had improved, and escape was possible if we acted boldly. Our pan had been swept over towards what seemed to be the river's opposite bank. Perhaps 150 metres (492 ft.) of compressed slush separated us from that bank (which was, of course, merely another, much larger, and hopefully more stable pan). Once again all movement seemed to have slowed and almost stopped. We broke camp in record time, bolted some food, and prepared to make a new assault on the river.

At first glance, its surface seemed to be a cohesive whole, but we knew that the individual blocks and smaller pieces of ice were held together only by pressure from the larger floes. How long would they remain firm enough for us to walk on? We had only one chance to make our way to safety – we couldn't afford to shuttle back and forth. We started out, with backpacks and sleds, afraid that the river would churn into life again beneath our feet. It took us two hours to inch our way across the narrow gap. Finally, we felt the surface change. It became smoother, less jumbled – then covered with ordinary snow. We knew that we were marching now on a normal ice floe – that we'd somehow managed to ford that devilish river.

It seems that we were too keyed up to stop; we pressed on with the rest of the working day. We moved across a wide expanse of even rougher ice that seemed to have been forced through a giant meat-grinder. Jagged blocks had been frozen in fantastic and incredible positions. Another white-out fell. The milky fog made the ice appear unnaturally blue; the snow cover seemed to be saturated with a diffused, dull, and very unpleasant light. A sense of hostility and intangible menace hung in the air – the sort of feeling that would make your flesh creep if you were locked inside a strange and darkened room. Logically, you know that the room is empty, but you begin to imagine mysterious rustlings in the corners, terrible monsters that will jump out from underneath the bed.

We walked amid this silent white world, devoid of shadow. Everything around us lost all recognizable dimension and became flat. We never knew when our feet would meet the surface; we could not discern either near or far perspective. A block of ice that seemed, judging by its outlines, to be rather small might turn out to be twice or three times as large when we drew close to it. A sense of all-pervasive isolation weighed heavily upon us. Nothing could dispel or brighten the surrounding gloom. How fortunate we were to have each other! Neither of us could imagine how a solo traveller would fare, thrown back entirely on his own resources.

But then the ice's character changed again, as if we'd crossed some invisible boundary separating two quite different parts of the ocean. These sudden transformations were likely to continue as long as we remained above the Lomonosov Ridge. Here, 180 miles (333 km) from land, the ocean was quite shallow – a depth of 1,000 metres (3,280 ft.). That fact, combined with a strong wind, had helped to produce the ice river. But never mind. We had survived its grasp, which gave us new strength as we kept on marching in efforts to make camp at a safe distance.

MAY 14-15 (DAY FIFTY-NINE). Last night we received another disturbing radio message – this time Jean read us a letter from Liane. She reiterated that First Air will not make a pickup on the ice later than May 28 and again exhorted us to make a dash for the Pole, taking three weeks' food. Now that we've had time to think her suggestion through, we see that three weeks will put us well past May 28 and into June. This casts doubt on First Air's ultimatum. She also advised that an evacuation by Canadian military helicopters based in Alert (to the east of Cape Columbia) will cost $100,000; that there is no money in the expedition account; and that if we made it as far as the Pole, our sponsors would consider the journey a success, because their primary concern is for our safety and well-being.

MAY 16 (DAY SIXTY). During our ninth march, we once again entered a field of severely broken ice. Digging deep into his inexhaustible supply of Russian proverbs, Misha said, "The eyes are afraid, but the hands will work." It's easy to lose heart, but you must simply make a start and continue step by step until the obstacle is overcome. We take comfort in the notion that conditions on the way back cannot possibly be any worse than those we've already experienced and survived. We have sufficient food and supplies; we have the will to continue. Only we have the knowledge on which to base our decisions; only we have the right to make them and to press on to the end.

MAY 18 (DAY SIXTY-TWO). Another day of rest, which we put to good use by rechecking our provisions and verifying that we have enough food to reach the Pole and return to Ward Hunt. Richard transmitted two radio messages: the first, to Josée, urging her to stop worrying, because everything is going according to plan; the second, to Liane, telling her that her task as manager is to present us with facts, not to arrange solutions, especially anything concerning our sponsors. But Josée's own message, when it arrived, was extremely grim. She seems to have lost all confidence in the expedition and feels that we are in pursuit of an illusory goal. When he got this message, Richard remained silent for a very long time. Nothing that Misha could say was of the slightest use. The only thing to do was to get to our feet and walk forward.

MAY 20-21 (DAY SIXTY-FOUR). By the end of the day, the sun began to shine, transforming our surroundings if not our mood. The ice ceased to look so daunting, becoming once again our everyday, familiar environment. We call it our "office," and every morning, like any other commuter, we shake ourselves awake, stumble out the door, and go to work.

But there are other commuters en route. For two marches, we followed the traces of an Arctic fox, which had left pawprints in the fresh snow and clawmarks on the edges of the cracks. The fox was heading north with unerring accuracy. Having detoured around an obstacle, it would immediately seek out a true bearing. It might have been breaking trail for us. Each time it needed to cross a rough area, it chose the best available path. Eventually we lost the tracks, where the fox crossed ice too thin for us to follow.

MAY 21-22 (DAY SIXTY-FIVE). In thirteen hours, we covered another 10.8 miles (19.9 km) and reached a latitude of 86°56'. We drifted north during the previous night, thanks to a southerly wind. On one lead with thin ice, the crust was elastic, and bent beneath our weight. It wobbled in oddly wavelike patterns; we felt as if we were walking across a waterbed.

MAY 23 (DAY SIXTY-SIX). Today's radio link was very poor, but Jean read a letter from Richard's father, Hans, who described the situation that lay ahead, as far as he could determine it by means of ice drift information and recent overflights. He felt that we would be able to reach the Pole, but not to return, because of an increasingly strong drift eastward in the direction of Greenland.

Another message was even more unsettling. Jean reported that the RCMP had notified us that our expedition was "intentionally placing itself in a situation whereby a rescue will be required" and that they would therefore "accept no responsibility for its removal, transport, or supply." They said that we had been duly advised by "knowledgeable sources" that continuing "at this late date" might place us in peril and urged that we "reconsider our motives." In other words, if we had to be picked up and flown out, it would be our own fault, and our own financial burden.

How tired we are of this ceaseless bad news! For her part, Josée felt that Richard had become obsessed, "gambling too high" with his life and their future together. Every radio contact pours salt on open wounds; we begin to dread the very prospect. Both of us had trouble falling asleep; and for the first time, Richard asked Misha to give him a sedative. All night the wind raged with such strength that we feared it would carry away the tent, and a remote groaning reached our ears — the sound of distant ice floes in accelerated motion.

MAY 26 (DAY SIXTY-NINE). This evening we debated the options for our evacuation, should things come to that. The $100,000 figure appears to refer to not one but two helicopters, flying from Alert to the Pole and back. But if we ourselves made a turnaround at the Pole and then headed south, the cost should decrease; the closer we get to Ward Hunt, the cheaper the flights. We need more information and more hard numbers on the costs of flights to various latitudes. As for alternatives, Hans had offered a dissenting opinion on the question of a post-May 28 pickup by plane. In his view, a Twin Otter should be able to land on the ice until mid-June. We'd placed $20,000 on deposit with First Air, guarding against the possibility of a just such a flight. Surely this remains a viable option, and we will ask Liane to clarify the situation.

MAY 27-28 (DAY SEVENTY). The previously benevolent drift
pattern has begun to work against us. We lost a mile (1.8 km)
overnight. Hans's forecast was accurate: we are drifting towards
the Greenland Sea. This threatens to bring our efforts to naught
– but, once again, there is nothing we can do about it. Nor can
Richard confront, at this distance, the problems that beset him.
Josée's messages continue to trouble his mind. Each of us is
absorbed in his own thoughts, and Richard looks not at the ice,
not at the pressure ridges, but inward. He seems to be striving to
solve a complicated puzzle whose pieces refuse to form a coher-
ent whole.

Is it possible that we will be forced to abandon the journey?
And if so, what will our friends and sponsors think; what will we
ourselves think if we abandon the task? We cannot turn back
until we have done our best, and now is not the time to give up
hope. No mortal danger threatens us, only the inexorable passage
of time and the insidiously shifting ice.

In the morning, we agreed to continue, to reach the Pole if at
all possible, then to make our way back and cover as much
distance as we can, thus lessening the cost of a rescue flight.
Tonight we will repack our supplies into one backpack and one
sled each. We transmitted a message, asking that Liane determine
whether we can be airdropped an inflatable boat. That would
spell an end to our unsupported status, but we at least could
attempt to get back to Ward Hunt on our own.

In fifteen hours, we covered only 5.5 miles (10.2 km). The ice is
uneven and terribly broken up. We are surrounded by leads and
cracks. But today's radio contact was more hopeful: First Air
declares that they are prepared to pick us up at any point south
of the Pole, as long as we assure them that they can land on the
ice without risk. Their pilots report that this is the roughest ice
in fifteen years. No one can say that our timing hasn't been
impeccable.

At day's end, we abandoned two of our sleds. It's like losing old friends; we'd named them all, in keeping with their appearance and personalities. Richard called his first sled "Jim," and Misha had christened his "Arnold." This referred to bulk: the real-life namesakes were men of imposing girth. Our second sleds both bear the same name, which we need not record. This person has seen stumbling blocks even where none existed, bumping against imaginary obstacles and causing us no end of trouble.

JUNE 1 (DAY SEVENTY-FOUR). The first day of Arctic summer — but here we sit amid a violent snow squall. We walked for thirteen hours, but progressed only 8.1 miles (14.9 km). Two weeks ago, with a much heavier load, we averaged eleven miles (20 km) a day. But better news comes at last during our radio contact. Josée's spirits have risen, and she promises to spend Richard's birthday, which fast approaches, on a camping trip with their sons. As well, Liane reports that the expedition accounts show a balance of $50,000 — enough to cover the cost of evacuation by military helicopters. The Russians have made a sort of competing bid: a helicopter unit based on Sredny Island (just off the Siberian coast) is prepared to fly us out for $23,000. We also learn that another team of Norwegians who'd started off from Russia are now past the Pole and heading down towards us. They, too, are fighting the eastward drift and have arranged to be picked up by First Air.

JUNE 2-3 (DAY SEVENTY-FIVE). A narrow escape today. Richard was crossing a small crack, about a metre (3 ft.) deep, and had gained the far side when the edge crumbled and his sled crawled back into the dark water. He was on skis and could not gain a foothold to haul it out. Misha dashed along the crack, leapt across, and ran back to give him a hand. Together we managed to pull the sled onto the ice. One end was slightly waterlogged, but

most of the contents – and, more importantly, Richard himself –
remain unharmed.

JUNE 4 (DAY SEVENTY-SEVEN). A terrible weariness haunted
us throughout the day's marches. We fixed all our energies merely
on putting one foot in front of the other – pure survival, step by
step, and every step accomplished only by the exercise of sheer
will. We resembled draught horses, beasts of burden, but no
warm stable awaited us. Our breathing grew laboured and heavy;
the sharp wind drove us to despair. But then, during a rest break,
the wind shifted to the south. If it holds, it will propel us northward. We are within eighty miles (148 km) of the Pole. We calculate that we will need at least another week, perhaps two, to reach
the top of the planet. But it's useless to look too far ahead; we are
at the mercy of the wind.

JUNE 5-6 (DAY SEVENTY-EIGHT). Today we decided to count
the cracks, but became bored with this exercise after we'd crossed
over forty-one of them. Visibility was very poor; we constantly
stumbled into unseen obstacles, probing ahead with our ski
poles, wasting valuable time. A successful return to Ward Hunt
is still possible, but with every hour's delay, our chances become
slimmer.

JUNE 7-8 (DAY EIGHTY). We grow weaker day by day. Strangely,
a stretch of flat ice induces even more numbing tedium; we almost
welcome the appearance of a crack – a challenge that interrupts
our dogged and plodding rhythm, forcing us to concentrate and
work even harder. We succeed in covering another 12.7 miles (23.5
km), and have reached 88°51' – so near, yet so far. Even our dreams
are filled with thwarted hopes. Misha's involve his attempts to eat
something, which are constantly blocked by various interruptions.
Richard's are even more explicit. He goes with his family to a

restaurant in search of pizza — but when they arrive, the place is closed, and they remain hungry.

JUNE 9 (DAY EIGHTY-ONE). Today is Richard's birthday — he is thirty-three. His only present, alas, is a chocolate bar, which we divide and eat with our morning coffee. We are drifting southward an average of three miles (6 km) daily. Were it not for the wind, we'd be very close to the Pole by now. As it is, there are fifty-five miles (102 km) to go. The Norwegians have been picked up in the vicinity of 88°5', so we are now the only game in town.

JUNE 10-11 (DAY EIGHTY-TWO). Forty-three miles (80 km) to the Pole.

JUNE 11-12 (DAY EIGHTY-THREE). For sixteen hours straight, we battle wet snow, terrible ice, and a southwesterly wind that pushes us eastward by six miles (11 km). During our seventh march, we encounter a 100-metre-wide (328-ft.-wide) lead and climb atop a pressure ridge to see if we can spot a crossing place. But none is evident, and we walk along the lead through rain and icy hail until it narrows. We find a floating block of ice that serves as a makeshift bridge. During one of the rest breaks, a seal appeared, lazily padding along another lead. We decided not to shoot it, but perhaps we shall regret our decision. The possibility that we will run short of food grows with each delay. But we work for fourteen hours and arrive at 89°33' — 8.2 miles (15.2 km) closer to the Pole.

JUNE 12-13 (DAY EIGHTY-FOUR). For the first time, we made no forward progress. By mid-afternoon, we'd reached 89°38'. When we camped for the night, we'd drifted back to 89°36'. Tomorrow morning we shall be back where we started from. We're marching in place, accomplishing nothing at all.

JUNE 14 (DAY EIGHTY-FIVE). We have drifted southward during the night to 89°34'. A new storm seems to be blowing up as we prepare to set off again. Our progress is minuscule; we end the day at 89°39' – twenty-one miles (39 km) short of the Pole. To have any hope of returning to Ward Hunt before the ice breaks up, we must turn back now. Perhaps we could reach the Pole in two or three more days; but perhaps not. We might march in fractions of a mile for a week or more, driving ourselves to exhaustion and consuming most of our food. The ice is broken past all belief, riddled with 100- and 200-metre-wide (328- and 656-ft.-wide) leads. It takes hours to skirt one, during which time we're blown even farther back and off to the side. Our time has run out, and we must make a dash for the south.

CHAPTER NINE

JUNE 15 (DAY EIGHTY-SIX). This is as far as we shall get, this year at least. We might have fought the ice and open water for another few days – but, having done so, we'd have had no hope of making it back to land. That slim chance still exists; we must fix our minds on this new goal. We are so very close, by anyone's reckoning. At all events, our journey is now the longest unsupported expedition on record.

But first, before we headed southward, we had to go west, to 65° longitude. We'd drifted east to a longitude of almost 30°. Had we tried to march straight south from there, we'd have ended up in Ireland. The wind was in our faces; every step became an ordeal. There was no end to the shifting mass of snow, the numberless cracks, and ever-widening leads.

During our radio contact, our friends endorsed our decision

and congratulated us on coming so close. A plane with our film crew on board flew above us, so low that we could see Pat Doyle at the controls. One person was wearing a short-sleeved shirt. The plane dropped a parcel containing our sponsors' flags and a new videocamera; ours had given up the ghost, back before the ice river. We were in radio contact with the plane and were cheered to learn that the ice to the south was not as bad as we'd feared. But this, as we knew all too well, could change overnight. We will have to cover fifteen miles (28 km) a day for twenty-four days if we hope to reach Ward Hunt before our food is gone.

JUNE 16 (DAY EIGHTY-SEVEN). The eastward drift continues unabated. Although we made our planned fifteen miles (28 km), we know in our hearts that the drift can't be overcome. We send a message via TUBSAT expressing our thanks to everyone who believed in and supported us.

JUNE 17 (DAY EIGHTY-EIGHT). We ski into a ferocious head-wind through sleet and wet snow. We make only five miles (9 km) to the south.

JUNE 18-19 (DAY EIGHTY-NINE). The situation is coming to a head. We are back at 89°, but during the first four marches, we ran into a lead or crack every 100 metres (328 ft.). The Arctic was melting around us. We heard, and later saw, a pair of whales that surfaced in one of the leads. (No one has ever reported whales in the middle of the Arctic Ocean — the farthest north has been between Greenland and Ellesmere Island. We should have known that we were in trouble, because whales progress from crack to crack as they must breathe air. This meant that the ice was completely broken all the way to land.) During the eighth march, confronted by yet another gigantic lead, we realized that we could not make it back to Ward Hunt. We had food for only twenty-two days. Judging by our southward progress thus far, we'd take more than twice that long. By then it would be August; we'd be swimming our way to shore. We could request an air-dropped boat – but that would aid us only in crossing the largest leads. Besides, the banks of many leads are two metres (7 ft.) high. Try launching and disembarking from an inflatable boat under those conditions. And what if the boat were to puncture or malfunction? In July no ordinary plane could land on the ice; we'd be forced to summon the helicopters, which might have to pluck us from the open sea. Surely our wisest course is to call for a flight at once and spend the next day or two making our way to a place where the ice is solid enough for First Air to touch down.

Suddenly we realized how tired we'd become. We rounded the lead, but felt no joy; we knew that all our struggles were in vain.

Time had defeated us at the outset. On March 13, the moment we'd stepped onto the pack ice off Ward Hunt, we knew that we were cutting things a bit fine. The original start date was February 23. The snowstorm had delayed us for five days. Then we'd been slowed by Bob and his komatiks, blown every which way by the wind, stymied by horrendous ice, and marooned on the ice river. So many factors have combined to conspire against us, while good luck has been conspicuous only by its absence.

JUNE 19-20 (DAY NINETY). In the morning, Misha was sleeping like a child, but Richard had spent a restless night, replaying the expedition in his mind. Would we be able to summon up the courage to make another attempt? Could we live with ourselves if we didn't venture one more try?

JUNE 20 (DAY NINETY-ONE). Today, according to our original plan, we should have been walking up to the huts on Ward Hunt Island. Instead we drifted two miles (4 km) south and another two miles (4 km) east. It's time to call a halt.

During our radio contact, we informed Jean of our decision.

Next we threw caution to the wind and gorged ourselves on the remaining food. We ate indiscriminately; there is no need for rationing anymore. We put a whole teaspoon of coffee in our cups, then threw in enough powdered milk to bridge a small lead. Café au lait and biscuits slathered in peanut butter! — our first and last indulgence of the trip.

JUNE 21. We spent our final day on the ice looking for a suitable landing strip. The weather was beautiful, sunny and windless, as if the Arctic had decided to wave farewell — or, perhaps, thumb its nose at two uninvited guests who'd overstayed their welcome.

We sat leaning against our backpacks, basking in the sun and talking about the next time — which was already assuming its own reality in our minds. The First Air flight was due in several hours. We wandered around amid the pressure ridges, clearing a landing strip with our shovel.

We heard the aircraft's approach, but just as we'd sighted it, it disappeared amid the clouds. Misha climbed a pressure ridge and began to wave the bright-red floor panel of our tent. We weren't in direct contact with the pilot; instead, Richard kept shouting into the radio transmitter, and Jean, in Resolute, relayed our sometimes frantic instructions to the cockpit.

"Tell them to turn left!" Misha yelled from high atop his slippery perch. No sooner had Richard repeated this than the plane veered right. "To the sun!" cried Misha. "Tell them to fly into the sun!"

Jean, confused by these opaque transmissions, asked us if we were in the fog. "I can't see where they are," said the pilot. "But we're in fog, and we can't land."

The trouble, we learned, was that the co-pilot was trying to reconcile our directions with the reading on his new GPS unit, and had managed to get everything reversed, which is why the plane kept taking precisely the opposite course. But in a minute or so, we gained contact with the plane, which in fact flew into the sun – enabling the crew to see us and locate the landing strip. The plane circled above us and made two passes over the area we'd shovelled clear. On the second run, its skis tentatively brushed along the surface, but then it took off again. Our hearts sank: perhaps the crew had decided that they couldn't land after all and would fly back to Resolute, taking with them our $20,000 fee.

But in a moment, having spotted a better-looking strip, they made a third approach, and came to a halt about a kilometre (0.6 miles) away from where we stood. A range of pressure ridges blocked our view; we could see only the tip of the plane's tail. "I hope there isn't an open lead between us," Misha said. "There are probably two or three," Richard replied, unable to believe that even the slightest luck would hold.

In fact, there were four or five, but we made our way across them to the landing strip. The co-pilot introduced himself. "Hello," he said, "I'm Benoit, from Montreal." We hadn't met, but to our delight, his companion, the pilot, was our old friend Karl Zeberg, who'd worked with Will Steger's expedition, with Polar Bridge, and with Icewalk. We knew that we were in good hands.

Flying southward, we saw for ourselves that we'd made the right decision. Two narwhals frolicked in a vast expanse of open water. As far as the eye could see, the white surface was cut with thousands of cracks. After we'd passed 87°, the ocean became more fluid by the mile – a semi-frozen gruel that looked like our breakfast porridge. If we'd continued on foot, no power on earth could have brought us safely to the shores of Ward Hunt at that time of year.

CHAPTER TEN

Contrary to popular belief, we didn't swear a blood oath to come back and beat the Arctic into submission. We wanted to return, and we had a fair idea what had gone wrong with our first attempt. But there were one or two obstacles of another sort to be overcome before we could seriously contemplate a second kick at the can.

In the first place, we needed another $200,000. As for what we'd done wrong, that was simple enough. We left too late; and, with the wisdom of hindsight, there ought to have been just the two of us. Everything else was a detail. We thought about minor changes to our equipment and diet; we knew that we'd probably get rid of the radio and depend entirely on satellite communication. But that was about the extent of it. We never even considered for a moment the idea of looking for a third or fourth person to accompany us. Nor was there any question of now attempting a round-trip from the Russian side or of crossing from Russia to Canada (like Polar Bridge, but unsupported). It was suggested to us that this second approach was farther, and therefore a greater accomplishment. We knew differently. Though it is more miles to cross the ocean than to go from Canada to the Pole and back, the two routes cannot be compared. On the Russian side, the ice is flatter and the drift much more favourable. A few extra miles would be a small price for such good ice. No, if we crossed the ocean, we still would not have been satisfied until we completed the round-trip from the Canadian side. We knew that when we came back, we'd simply retrace our steps. The trick was to do it right the second time around.

We didn't believe that we'd be able to do it until 1995, so we started counting down to that date. We had to unwind, regroup, get our sponsors onside, and confirm our funding sources. The first few weeks were spent thanking everyone who'd helped us. Misha delayed his departure for Russia so that we could visit all concerned. We were delighted to find that the most frequent reaction was "So, when are you going to do it again?"

It didn't take long to wind down the first expedition. Suffice to say that we weren't a red-hot item on the speakers circuit. The media had paid plenty of attention to Bob's misadventures – but when we got home, we were just another couple of might-have-beens. We felt pretty good about ourselves. We'd done our best and come back alive, which was a plus. We were the only people in history to have reached the Pole three times; we'd spent more time unsupported on the ice than anybody else. All of which, with a ticket, got us aboard a bus. So, in terms of fame and more particularly fortune, it was back to square one.

The rest of our little group dispersed in various directions. Jean's job was finished, Vasiliy stayed put in Russia, and Liane went on to other things. John had long since returned to Outward Bound, and Bob was in the process of moving to Iqaluit (but would later go back to the United States and drop out of sight). By the way, we didn't even bother contacting Dick Smith, the altruistic Australian. We hadn't met the terms and conditions of his offer, so there wasn't a lot to say.

Which meant that we had to scramble for money. In 1993, we signed a two-year consulting contract with Kaufman Footwear. That was something to bank on, but not enough – and so we decided to launch North Pole Light.

Our plan (which had first popped into Richard's mind back at the time of the Global Concern balloon flights) was to offer people the ultimate adventure tour. We'd fly them to within 100 kilometres (62 mi.) of the Pole, then ski the final distance in short and relatively easy stages, camping on the ice. Our approach would be from the Russian side – as we've said, that's by far the less difficult route. The trips would take place during late April and early May, when the weather is as good as it gets. The sun's up all the time; you can see where you're going, and the tent stays reasonably warm. If you'd had any experience with winter camping and cross-country skiing, it wouldn't be beyond your power. A working day would be limited to five or six hours – during which time, we thought that we could cover an average of half a dozen miles (11 km). It would be a real expedition, just not so long or cold.

When it came to rounding up prospective clients, advertising didn't really avail; we weren't talking about an impulse purchase. Nor were we talking about bargain-basement cost. The first two expeditions, both of which took place in 1993, cost about $12,500 (Can.) all-inclusive. You turned up with a change of underwear, a pair of sunglasses, and your backpack. Everything else was provided – your clothing, skis, food, and air transportation. The flights were something of an adventure in themselves. Our first tours left from Russia; Misha and his seemingly infinite network of business contacts had matters well in hand. But the Russian system takes its toll on entrepreneurs. It was difficult if not downright impossible to get a firm price on anything at all until the week before departure. Dealing with Aeroflot in Dikson, in Siberia, was particularly frustrating. Misha's assistant had to go there two or three times and engage in marathon vodka-drinking contests in order to nail down a contract.

But we persevered, and in the end everything went well. The first party flew to Moscow and was taken by bus to Ryazan, where Misha had arranged for them to stay in local people's apartments. Then they were flown to Dikson, to Sredny, and then by helicopter to a latitude of 89°. They advanced to the Pole, where they were picked up by another helicopter, which had meanwhile dropped the second group back at the starting point. At least one of us was on hand at all times to guide everybody across the ice.

Who were the valiant customers? The first bunch looked rather like old-home week. Besides three Canadians from the Ottawa area, Ken Hossack, Kent Humphrey, and Mark Fuller, it included Peter Green (the president of Alcatel) and his son, James; our fellow explorer Robert Swan and his companion, Nicky Cole; Paul Lavelle, who'd organized the Global Concern balloon flights; Vladimir Mazaev, the president of the PRIO Bank in Ryazan, who'd been one of Misha's personal sponsors, and Ivan Troffimov, a Mexican who wanted to gain experience so he could make his own North Pole expedition. The second group was put together by Anthony Willoughby, who runs an outdoor adventure company in Japan. He'd previously introduced Swan to the Amway Corporation, which resulted in that firm's sponsorship of Icewalk. This time he rounded up several Japanese, a number of western businessmen based in Tokyo, and Jerry Corr, an American.

So far, so good. In October 1993, we were invited by Peter Monk, the president of Paris Gloves, another of our corporate sponsors, to make a presentation to ExPO, the alumni membership of the Young Presidents Organization. During this event, we met Michel Perron. Although only sixty-one years old, he was semi-retired, having been a major force in the Canadian forest products industry. Earlier in the year, he'd become extremely ill and had received a kidney transplant from his son Henri. He was on the mend, though, and when he saw the film we'd made during our first expedition, he said, "Wow! I want to do that; I'd like to join you." This was unusual by anyone's standards, and Misha advised him to consult his doctor. The doctor, although almost certainly nonplussed, said, "Well, you've had the transplant, and you're supposed to be as good as new — so why not go ahead?"

Which is how Michel, who months earlier had been staring down a death sentence, started training to become a polar explorer.

He also roped in everybody he could think of – including Bertrand, another of his sons, and his nephew Richard; Tim Kenny, then sixty-four, another forest products executive; Gerard Lebeau, a sixty-six-year-old auto parts manufacturer; and Pierre Simard, who was in his fifties. The group also included Tim Goodsell, a Chicago banker; Robert Owen, a Britisher who worked with a Tokyo brokerage house; and Jeff Mantell, a New York-based commodities broker.

By this time, our Russian friends had grasped the virtues of rampant capitalism and had jacked up all the prices. As a result, the third trip cost the participants $12,500 (U.S.). But this did not deter the group, even though the weather – which had been ideal the previous year – turned nasty towards the end of the journey. We modified the schedule to suit the fact that three of the travellers had waved goodbye to sixty. Gerard was perhaps the most excited of them all; he'd never been in a tent in all his life, let alone a sleeping bag. We spread the weight around in keeping with Marxist dogma: from each according to his abilities. Rob Owen, for example, was gung-ho; we loaded up his sled and away he went, although suffering mightily from allergies that flared up when he was bitten by bedbugs in his Moscow hotel room. As we've just mentioned, the weather decided to snap cold at the end: $-30°C (-22°F)$ and strong winds. We were back in our element, but Michel had to pace himself with care, and spent some of the trip skiing quietly along, sometimes without even a pack. Just being there was accomplishment enough.

Whenever we talk about North Pole Light, we always come back to Michel's experiences. The previous year, his days were numbered; at his age, he wasn't a prime candidate for a transplant. But he got one, thanks to his son's supreme generosity, and before you could turn around, he was skiing to the Pole. We celebrated his sixty-second birthday on the ice. It's no exaggeration to say that the trip changed his life. He'd been thinking about reviving a disused pulp and paper mill at Port-Cartier, Quebec, but had hit a brick wall when it came to financing the project. Potential lenders had said, basically, "You're dying, and so is Port-Cartier. You're a sick old man; rest in bed and drink plenty of fluids." After he came back from the Pole, they didn't say that anymore. Today, both he and the mill are up and running. He single-handedly raises huge amounts of money for the Kidney Foundation; nothing can stand in his way. According to his friends who've known him for many years, he's a whole new person. Michel's is a very special case — but all of the other participants were changed as well. The trip made them stronger in all sorts of ways. They know what they'd succeeded in doing on the polar ice, and life's minor stumbling blocks tend to pale by comparison.

Meanwhile, however, we had a major stumbling block to consider — the fact that we had to close the circle, to go back and accomplish what we'd stopped short of doing.

If we didn't, someone else would. The media might have lost interest to some degree, but the polar fraternity had taken note of how close we'd come. In 1994, we heard that two more Norwegians were going to make an unsupported round-trip attempt. At first we thought that they were the same pair who'd come close to succeeding one-way in 1990. Those guys were tough; if they put their minds to it, they stood a decent chance. Worse yet, they were planning to follow our route exactly. Our preparations were far from complete, and we feared that they'd beat us to the punch. Misha was so wary that he visited Norway and checked them out. He came back much relieved. These were two fresh talents, and Misha telephoned with welcome news. "Don't worry," he said.

"They won't make it." This proved to be yet another example of his ability to get an instant fix on strangers. In this case, he was quite right, and the rival expedition floundered on the ice not far from Ward Hunt Island.

So we continued on our schedule. During the summer of 1994, we'd met a young woman named Deb Hine, who signed on as a part-time aide, but then was promoted to expedition manager. She began to compile a voluminous mailing list and produced a newsletter that, along with weekly fax transmissions, would keep the world abreast of our activities. Deb was assisted by Tim Kenny, who declared that he wanted to be an unpaid coordinator, on call and on hand if the wheels came off. Not to be outdone, Paul Lavelle, who was by that time living in Norway, signed on as an unpaid adviser. He, too, would be invaluable if a crisis arose. We presented our campaign plan to him in exhaustive detail. He studied it up, down, and sideways, then said that he didn't know if it would work, but that he couldn't see anything wrong with it.

Josée was back on board as well, albeit reluctantly. The 1992 expedition had been difficult for her. There was a period when people were telling her that her husband and his friend were crazy, and the RCMP were threatening her with huge search-and-rescue costs. The RCMP even suggested having us declared legally insane so that they could go and snatch us off the ice. Every time she went out in public, she knew people were thinking, "Poor Josée, stuck at home with two young children while her irresponsible husband is losing his mind somewhere near the North Pole." So she was not jumping for joy at the suggestion of another expedition. But as a former athlete, she understood about setting goals, and she understood the importance of such an undertaking.

Josée did not have much to look forward to during the upcoming expedition, almost six months by herself, minimum income, and a lot of stress concerning her husband's welfare. She also had to put any of her personal plans and ambitions on hold for another two years. To her credit, she stood behind us. She supported us quietly in the background, sewing, running errands, talking to sponsors, and looking after the family and the home. And there is an exciting aspect to the expeditions that she does like. At least life is never boring.

Peter and Tom Mateuzels were also back, and well suited to handle our media relations. Peter worked with the Canadian freestyle ski team and Tom worked for the CBC. All of our corporate sponsors gathered round, with the sole exception of Alcatel, because Peter Green had since left the company. But he helped us with very generous personal donations – as did Michel Perron, without whom the second expedition would have been almost impossible to mount. Indeed most of the members of the 1994 North Pole Light tour stepped forward with generous contributions to the expedition: Gerard Lebeau, Pierre Simard, Tim Kenny, Jeff Mantell, Richard Perron, and Michel's brother, Jean Perron.

One more aspect of the expedition should be mentioned here. In 1992, we'd made an arrangement with TVOntario, the province's educational network, whereby public and high-school students could watch a program that updated our progress, then phone in and send us questions via radio. That was fine, but we thought we could do a much better job by making use of TUBSAT and the Internet.

Back when we were getting ready for the first expedition, we'd established an E-mail link between Ottawa's Confederation High School and a number of Russian students in Ryazan. John Hindel, a science teacher, was the guiding force behind this early effort. In 1994, we contacted him and principal John Spence. That was the genesis of Project Follow Us. Very simply, the idea was that we would send and receive messages via TUBSAT, which could be downloaded and accessed by 260 sites worldwide.* Actually, there were considerably more participants; several schools could share a single classroom's site. To join in, each school had to devise an activity for the students to perform. For example, they might choose to tow a 165-kilogram (364-lb.) sled around the block for hours on end. Others might engage in somewhat less strenuous lab work – but everyone could submit questions to Confederation High, via the Internet. We'd pre-answered about 200 of the more predictable queries or figured out which resources would have to be tapped in order to come up with an answer. Anything out of the ordinary could be relayed to us, and we'd reply as best we could. As a result, several thousand students in nine countries would be able to chart (and feel a part of) our daily progress. It should be noted that all our communications would be handled by the teenaged students at Confederation High School. No one else would have another TUBSAT transceiver. They proved to be very professional and dedicated, providing the best communications of any expedition we ever experienced – simple and effective.

---

* To send a message, you scroll through the alphabet, which appears on a tiny one-line screen at the top, and stop at the first letter you want to send. Then you do the same for the next letter, and so on. The unit will send or receive a maximum of sixty-four characters, so messages are necessarily terse. You have one-letter codings for the recipient, the progress you're making, the weather conditions, the approximate temperature, and so on. For example, a message might read: "C [progress satisfactory]. E [mild cloud, mild wind]. M [temperature is −38°C (−36°F)]. 83 d 24 m n. 74 d w. [location expressed in latitude and longitude]." Next you punch in whatever else you want to convey. Things get confusing when you start omitting vowels to save space. For example, "Ice changing; like open ocean – excellent! Make depot tomorrow, Day 14" would be transmitted as: "Ice chngng lk opn ocen exclnt! mk depo tmrw day 14." When you're done, you review and save the message, then transmit it when the satellite is over-head. The unit makes a sound like a fax machine, and there you are. To receive a message sent by someone else, you punch "receive" when the satellite is passing by, and the message appears on the screen. We never used the TUBSAT in an emergency, but it would certainly serve that purpose. The only drawback is that each new message wipes out the preceding one (even on the satellite); its like re-recording a tape.

We didn't think of Project Follow Us as a fan club or cheering section; that would have trivialized the students' efforts. They were more like a support group – a network in the best sense – and it's wonderful that kids who were so young and previously inexperienced could take such an intense interest in two guys slogging their way across the middle of nowhere. You can read for yourself, in Appendix E, how splendidly they succeeded in their duties.

PART
TWO

CHAPTER ELEVEN

If our journal were a film script, this would be the place to call for an establishing (or perhaps a re-establishing) shot — pressure ridges and wind-swept ice floes stretching as far as the eye can see and a caption reading: "Two and a half years later."

It is early January 1995, and here we are again in Iqaluit. Our training sessions have already begun, out on Frobisher Bay. Very soon First Air will transport us north to Ward Hunt, and we'll set off for the Pole. We are 90 per cent certain that this time we will succeed both in reaching it and in returning to land — but no one can approach the Arctic with absolute assurance. It would be naive to suppose that our adversary will yield without a struggle.

This time around, we planned to leave on February 11 — much earlier than any previous expedition. We'd calculated that this would enable us to reach the Pole and return to Ward Hunt by the first or (at latest) the second week of June — well before the southern ice could turn to porridge beneath our feet. But so early a departure meant that we would at first be marching through the latter half of the long polar night. It wouldn't be absolutely dark, of course, but the days would be drastically shortened. How this would affect our progress was anyone's guess.

In Iqaluit we often trained in the dark to simulate polar night, but at least the comforts of home awaited us at the end of each training day. Our living quarters offered every amenity, including a television set and a microwave oven. We enjoyed them while we could; soon we would be crouched in a tent, communicating with the outside world by means of sixty-four-character TUBSAT transmissions.

There was another reason why we'd come north so early. We felt that it was necessary to distance ourselves from the pressures

and temptations of the world outside. In this way, we could focus
on our mission with a minimum of distraction. We quickly began
to feel as if the expedition had truly begun; we visualized and
anticipated each step of the coming adventure, weighing and
reweighing our load, packing and repacking our provisions. But
we found it unwise to limit ourselves strictly to each other's
company. This was our last opportunity to enjoy contact with
other humans before we would face the prospect of living alone
on the frozen ocean for four long months. Fortunately, we had
excellent companions – two young Japanese, Nobu Norita
(who'd joined us on the second North Pole Light tour) and
Atsushi Miyagawa. Now they were counting down to an expedition of their own. They planned to set off for the Magnetic Pole
in late February and were looking forward to making an attempt
on the Pole from Russia the following season. We found it pleasant to assume the role of Arctic mentors or senior statesmen –
particularly because both our pupils were intelligent, capable, and
quick to learn. Besides, when it came to cooking, they were quite
without equal.

One night Richard took his turn at preparing a festive meal.
The dining table was covered with fried chicken, corn salad, and
baked potatoes, all of which disappeared with lightning speed.
We felt as if we could eat no more – until our Japanese friends set
an enormous pot on the table and lifted the lid to release a
wonderful aroma. We weren't sure what the bubbling pot
contained, other than the inevitable quota of rice, but it was
certainly delicious.

FEBRUARY 2. The departure date is soon upon us. Darkness
reigns on the shores of Ward Hunt, which poses a problem for
the pilots who will fly us there. Ward Hunt is uninhabited, which
means that no one would be on the ground to clear, or at least
mark out, a landing strip with beacons and lights. But we'd

obtained a number of high-intensity flares from Thiokol Ltd., an American company that supplies the U.S. armed forces. These would be dropped by parachute, illuminating the ice below, which sounded better than the original idea – that a volunteer would parachute down and stand around tossing flares to all points of the compass. Each flare was about the size of a large cardboard mailing tube, but thicker – twenty centimetres (8 in.) in diameter by one metre (3 ft.) long. Each would burn for about five minutes, putting out 1.5 million candlepower. We'd been assured that each provided enough light so that a newspaper could be read half a mile (1 km) away. But so as to conserve our supplies, we hadn't actually tested the flares, and it quite literally remained to be seen how they'd perform.

We reviewed again the logistics of this journey – the main differences between our tactics now and back in 1992. This time, having established our base camp on Ward Hunt, our plan is to take half our supplies forward about ninety miles (167 km) to a latitude of 84°5' – the point at which we'd parted company with Bob Mantell – and establish a storage depot there. This, we estimated, would take us fourteen days, because we wouldn't be able to take all the equipment at once and would have to resort to shuttle marches. We'd mark the depot's location in two ways: with both an Argos beacon (that signals its position via satellite) and a Televilt homing device (a Swedish-designed unit that's used mainly to track migrating animals). Then we'd return to Ward Hunt and rest for a day or so, recovering our strength before we set off again with the remainder of our supplies.

The resting up is important. Travelling during polar night – when it's dark, with temperatures between −40°C (−40°F) and −55°C (−67°F) – is very hard on the body. At Ward Hunt we could take the advantage to rest properly and dry out our wet sleeping bags and clothes. The main drawback was that we might not be able to find the depot again amid the drifting ice – but that seemed unlikely; the ice that far south usually drifts relatively little until mid-March. Even if the depot wandered, we could find it again by means of the Televilt signals. The awful chance existed that a crack might open directly beneath the depot, plunging it forever to the bottom of the ocean, but this possibility seemed remote in the extreme.

Our expedition differed from 1992 in yet another way. As we marched north from Ward Hunt with the first half of our supplies, we planned to mark our pathway with signal flags – small black pennants attached to slim bamboo stakes, exactly the same sort you'd use to prop up flowers in your garden. These individually numbered flags would be mounted at intervals of a mile (2 km), if possible on the tops of pressure ridges, so that we'd be able to see them from a distance. Each time we planted one, we'd take a GPS reading and plot its exact location on our map. On our way back, we'd simply follow this (hypothetically) visible trail, taking further GPS readings as we went along. If the flags' positions had shifted, we'd know that the ice was drifting and could alter our course accordingly. Then we'd simply follow the flags again as we made our second haul northward to the food depot.

Sitting in Iqaluit, it seemed that we'd identified and reasoned through every conceivable detail, considering every possible variant and addressing every doubt. But the final proof awaits us still, out on the ocean of ice.

These imponderables gave rise to sometimes irrational behaviour. Shortly before we were to leave, we learned that a British explorer with the unlikely name of Og MacKenzie was planning to set off for the Pole shortly after we did. Details were scant; in fact, we'd never heard of him before. But we saw at once that we were going to confer on him an unexpected benefit. In the first place, we'll have marked the way for him – all he has to do is follow the flags. Secondly, depending on when he sets out, he might reach the depot while we are on our way back to Ward Hunt for the remainder of our supplies. Suppose that he rustles our food! We thought about spreading dire rumours to the effect that we'd mined or booby-trapped the depot (which we planned to do to scare away hungry polar bears). Richard went so far as to utter threats against poor MacKenzie, who'd never have dreamt of committing such a flagrant breach of polar etiquette. But paranoia strikes deep when you're dealing with life-or-death struggle. It's not a matter of things being blown out of proportion – merely that the proportions are very different. One day, during our first expedition, Misha accidentally spilled a mug of sport drink. This wasn't a problem; we weren't running short, and under any other circumstances, it would have been no big deal. But he fell into a black, almost-hysterical mood, and recriminated himself repeatedly. A mere trifle suddenly became an inconsolable loss. This sort of thing works in reverse, as well: a tiny sliver of smoked bacon rind seems like a sumptuous delicacy to be savoured and lingered over at inordinate length.

FEBRUARY 4. Today we welcomed Rick Sellick and other members of the Systems Engineering Society (SES). We'd met them the previous fall, and they'd touted the virtues of communicating via HEALTHSAT – a bigger and better version (or so they claimed) of TUBSAT. HEALTHSAT involves a Canadian polar-orbiting satellite. It has been used for several purposes – for example, to transmit medical information to Third World countries from Memorial University in Saint John, New Brunswick. HEALTHSAT's advantage is that you can transmit and receive a great deal of data at a time; you aren't limited to TUBSAT's hasty sixty-four-character notes. Rick Sellick and his colleagues at SES had designed and built a completely new portable system to work with the HEALTHSAT. But its major drawbacks are size and weight. The transmitting/receiving unit is in two parts: a palm-top computer with keypad and screen, and another transceiver about half again as large as a loaf of bread. The antenna was far too bulky and tipped the scales at four kilograms (9 lb.), so Rick and his colleagues have designed one that can be assembled from the bamboo poles, with wires intertwined. Presto! We are down to 300 grams (11 oz.) – but this new arrangement will have to be assembled and disassembled each time we want to get a message in or out, which might turn out to be counterproductive in the long run. As well, HEALTHSAT's hardware is relatively untested when it comes to extended use in extreme cold. Will it perform as advertised, out there in −40°C (−40°F)?

Well, it had better – and so had everything else. The house overflows with equipment; it threatens to engulf the living room. Our primary concern, as always, is reducing weight. This almost maniacal preoccupation may seem extreme, perhaps inconsequential. We've removed rolls of film from their canisters, cast aside every shred of unneeded packaging, and poured vitamins from their bottles into plastic bags. But out on the ice, a single gram assumes undue importance. Put enough of them together and they could slow our progress, spelling the difference between victory and defeat.

This year, for instance, we are armed to the teeth with a specially-modified rifle. The .357 magnum has gone to its reward; the RCMP, in their wisdom, decided that a handgun no longer offered adequate protection against bears, even though it was fine in 1992, and declined to issue us a permit. They also cited tougher Canadian gun laws. Perhaps they thought we might go on a rampage at the North Pole! Fortunately, Rick Sellick's neighbour, Dan Cullity, is a master gunsmith. He has taken apart a .308 Ruger and put it together again; shortening and hollowing out the stock and substituting an aluminum trigger guard. The end result weighs less than 2.5 kilograms (5.5 lb.) – extremely light for such a high-powered weapon.

We measure, weigh, and count every item. Despite our best intentions, each of our two loads, divided among two sleds and a single backpack, total 120 kilograms (265 lb.). Surely we have seen this movie before! And so the (only partially successful) attempt to reduce our burden starts all over again.

FEBRUARY 8. We departed Iqaluit for Resolute Bay, amid unseasonably warm weather. The temperature had risen from −30°C (−22°F) to 0°C (32°F) in the sun. This was plainly an aberration, but it gave us momentary pause: Would the thaw spread farther north and set the ice in motion? No fear. By the time we landed in Resolute, things had returned to worse than normal – hurricane winds accompanied by a reading of −38°C (−36°F).

We were scheduled to leave for Ward Hunt the following day, and settled down in our traditional stopover – the High Arctic International Hotel, located about ten kilometres (6 mi.) from the airport. We were having a meal when the owner, Basil Jesudason, brought us the latest weather reports – a sixty-three-kilometre-per-hour (40 mph) wind and −32°C (−26°F).

Basil (who has since passed away) was an unlikely person to bear such unwelcome and frigid tidings. He was born in India, but had lived in the Arctic for many years, and operated an outfitting business as well as the hotel. His wife, Terry, born in the Far North, told us that, a month or so earlier, she'd gone with Basil to visit his relatives in the steamy subcontinent. "It was hot as hell there," she said, "so in the end I told him to get us back home, because plus-forty was driving me mad." Resolute's temperature today was more than seventy degrees less than in Basil's homeland, and Terry was happy as a lark. In fact, it's almost as if

the day wasn't cold enough for her liking, and she offered us a
bowl of ice cream for lunch.

Basil and Terry were wonderful hosts. Everyone who headed
on to the Pole made a point of stopping over with them – surely
one of the world's most specialized "passing trades." The dining room walls were covered with photographs of confident-
looking explorers. Our pictures were there as well, along with a
pennant commemorating the 1988 Polar Bridge expedition,
which is when we first met our hosts. The shelves were crowded
with books written by our fellow adventurers. That night our
dinner was crowned by a fluffy white miracle of a cake, baked
specially by Terry to mark our visit. It was laden with calories
and, written in whipped cream, bore the message: "Good Luck
to Richard and Misha."

FEBRUARY 11. This is the day we'd planned to be underway. But,
to our dismay, the weather remains unchanged. There is no point
in leaving, even if we could: gale-force winds have closed the
runway at Eureka, our refuelling stop. Nothing is more vexing
than hanging about, going over the same fine-print details for
what seems like (and is) the hundredth time. We poked hopefully
at the sleds, continued to test the HEALTHSAT, and decided to
confront the issue of personal hygiene. Misha had declared that
since he had nothing better to do, he might as well have a trim.
Basil produced a pair of scissors and quickly reduced Misha's
pate to shining baldness. Richard smiled sympathetically; the top
of his head, at least, had long ago achieved this condition on its
own. Danny Kilabuk, the cameraman who will accompany us as
far as Ward Hunt, grinned broadly, pleased at having captured
the moment for posterity, and Misha took the opportunity to
lecture his captive audience. "The only creature who's going to
see me during the next four months is a polar bear," he said. "I
don't care how I look. I care how I'm going to feel. I am a doctor,

after all, and I assure you that the less hair I have, the more comfortable I'll be." Danny grinned even more broadly. "I don't mean insects," said Misha. "They don't live in such cold. They're not idiots like us. I mean only that our next shower will be some-time in the month of June! I don't want to itch all over. Take my word — the less hair, the better."

Hygiene on an Arctic expedition is almost non-existent. On rest days during the expedition, we would wash our faces and perhaps our private parts. The Arctic is not a dirty place, so not showering for four months wasn't so bad. We would change socks every few weeks and underwear perhaps once a month. But during the last two months of the expedition, we would not have rest days, so we only changed our socks. We actually finished the expedition with a clean set of long underwear; we carried it in case we went swimming.

At 4 A.M. we received a phone call from the airport; it seemed possible to fly. We hurled our gear into Basil's truck and went bumping down the road. At the airport, we shook Basil's hand and walked to our old friend the Twin Otter, equipped with skis so as to land on the ice at Ward Hunt. Our pilot was none other than Pat Doyle, chief pilot of First Air, who wanted to see for himself what the flares would do. Everyone piled in, and the plane took off — but scarcely was it aloft than the control tower notified us that we've managed to forget the bamboo aerial at Basil's hotel; he practically fell over it on his return and called the airport at once.

Without it, of course, we would be unable to make use of the HEALTHSAT — so back we went, retrieved the aerial, and took off again. A few minutes later, though, a lively conversation broke out among Pat, his co-pilot, and the on-board mechanic. The mechanic poked a screwdriver speculatively into what seemed to us a tangled maze of wiring. A generator had given up the ghost, and sparks flew in all directions — which was more than Pat was prepared for, and it was back to Resolute again, where a whole team of mechanics attacked the plane in order to identify and rectify the problem. We loitered inside the hanger, wondering if we'll be able to get airborne. But no such luck. After about an hour, it's plain that the breakdown will take too long to repair, and we're forced to retrace our route back to Basil's hotel.

FEBRUARY 12. Another day spent fiddling with our gear, which by this time we can pack and unpack blindfolded. (And just as well; that's exactly what we'll have to do during the polar night.) The weather is against us. The plane has been repaired, but now the airstrip at Eureka is closed because of harsh winds and heavy snow. Resolute, too, is getting hit by the storm; the snow's been falling for a solid twenty-four hours. Then, to our surprise, we receive another 4 A.M. wakeup call, informing us that conditions are about to moderate and that a truck is on its way to pick us up.

Misha had slept particularly badly, dozing for at the most a couple of hours. We struggled out of bed and completed our final packing – then sat and waited for almost an hour, with no sign of a truck. This began to prey on our nerves. Richard phoned the airport and was told that a second truck was on its way. Another truckless half-hour came and went. Basil attempted to rescue us by wheeling out a truck of his own, but we succeeded only in making our way a few hundred metres before we were blocked by massive drifts.

Only one option remained. We fired up Basil's snowmobile and attached a flat-bed wooden sled, onto which we tossed our gear. We hopped aboard and set off cross-country into a fifty-kilometre-per-hour (31 mph.) headwind in −38°C (−36°F). A fun start to our adventure, you must admit – and one that made the plane's ice-cold seats seem warm and comforting by comparison.

At last we were aloft, en route to Eureka, then onward to Ward Hunt. The plane was jammed with our supplies, and there was barely enough room for Lena Kashina, a Russian journalist, and Tim Goodsell, another friend and former North Pole Light participant, who had been helping us pack in Iqaluit. Danny trained his videocamera out the window, but very little could be seen below — only Ellesmere's gloomy mountain peaks, which looked like giant wrinkles on the face of the earth in the dim moonlight. All around us were black sky, black mountains, and dark-blue snow.

Finally, the approach to Ward Hunt began. Mike, the mechanic, was in the tail section and opened a hatch to admit the frigid wind. He tossed a flare into the void. It ignited at a preset altitude and drifted down, creating a huge and dazzling ball of yellow light. We tried to take photographs, jostling for position at the windows, but Pat, already distracted by the flare, shouted at us to stop it and sit down. We hid our cameras like schoolchildren caught in the act of a forbidden prank — but we couldn't resist the urge to capture the moment on film. The effect of the flare is difficult to describe: it wasn't "bright as day." We felt as if we were peering through a trapdoor into a darkened cellar by the light of a giant candle positioned halfway down the stairs. From below, it must have resembled an aerial bombardment. The glow lingered as the flare descended slowly and landed on the ground. It was more than sufficient for Pat to assess a good landing spot. Still, there wasn't a clearly delineated landing strip, and the whole operation was risky — but he brought it off with great aplomb, making it seem easy, like the veteran he is. So pleased was he with his success — and with our spontaneous applause when we touched down on the ice shelf — that he offered to taxi up closer to the hut, and brought us to a stop only a few hundred metres away.

We made our way to the hut with very little difficulty. The snow hadn't piled against it as badly as in 1992, and we were soon

inside. The crude structure seemed to have been frozen in time:
the same two beds, a table, a cooking-stove, a shelf with dog-
eared and woefully outdated books and magazines, and packs of
abandoned food. To us, it looked like home. Richard fired up the
generator and the room sprang to light, while Misha fetched
snow and began to boil it to make tea. By this time, Pat was even
more enthusiastic about the successful landing. "We've gained
valuable experience," he said. "Now we'll be much better equipped
to fly in the polar night. The flares may come in handy in other
emergency situations as well. As for you two, I haven't seen a traveller in twenty years who was better prepared. Well, it's time to say
goodbye. See you here in June! I hope not to see you while you're
on the march – no emergency flights this time around. Get back
on your own, and take good care of yourselves!" The others added
their own farewells, and then they all headed back to the plane. Pat
squeezed his considerable bulk into the cabin, taxied back along
the ice shelf, and in a few moments the plane was gone, lost to
sight as it gained altitude and disappeared into the black night,
leaving two lonely and uninvited guests behind.

We were excited by our sudden isolation – but not by the
rather mundane feeling of emptiness in our bellies, reminding us
that our day had begun at four in the morning back in Resolute.
To postpone unpacking our own supplies, we decided to raid the
larder, and dined that night on a mixed bag of ten- and twenty-
year-old foods left behind by Ranulph Fiennes and others. The
low point was buckwheat groats; where was Terry's baking now
that we really needed it?

FEBRUARY 13. Today we made two trial marches across the ice
shelf, moving our supplies towards our jumping-off point. It was
hard going in the pitch dark, but when the moon appeared above
the clouds, we were able to reacquaint ourselves with our
surroundings. Each of our sleds weighed fifty kilograms (110 lb.),

and we tried at first to pull two of them at once, as well as carry a backpack. By the end of the second march, we were quite worn out and feared that muscle cramps might set in at any moment. But we gained our second wind when we neared the edge of the ice shelf and saw the ocean before of us. We left our gear at 83°08' – three miles (6 km) offshore and far enough for the day. By 10 P.M. we were back at the hut, and turned in by midnight. The temperature outside was −50°C (−58°F). We agreed to sound reveille at six the following morning. Only then would we set foot on the pack ice and start counting off the 105 days of our expedition: to the Pole by May 10 and back to Ward Hunt by June 6.

CHAPTER TWELVE

FEBRUARY 14 (DAY ONE). We woke as planned at six o'clock, but spent the better part of four hours in final preparations. We must have looked for all the world like holiday-makers bound for a seaside resort – running mental checklists and taking last-minute stock of our possessions. We were convinced that we'd left nothing behind, but we were wrong. Long after we'd set off, Richard remembered that he'd forgotten his tape recorder and a serving cup.

We walked out to where we'd left our packs, and found them without difficulty. There was sufficient light in the sky; we didn't need to use our halogen lights, which are about the size of the head of an ordinary flashlight, fasten over our heads with nylon straps, and are powered by a lithium battery pack that we keep underneath our clothing. Unfortunately, our good luck vanished almost at once. The first patch of broken ice was every bit as bad as in 1992 and had received even more snow. Huge piles of jagged blocks were stacked ten to twelve metres (33 to 40 ft.) high, with deep ditches between. There were no pans at all to offer respite, not even a tiny, level surface. We forced our way through until we ran against an even higher pile; we christened it the Great Wall of China. We scouted along it in search of some semblance of a path. There was no way through; the only thing to do was to take the wall by storm. As we hauled the sleds up at a dizzying angle, we thought about Reinhold Messner, the renowned mountain climber, who intends to set off on a trans-Arctic journey, starting from Russia, sometime next month. He might do better when it comes to the ice walls — but not if he, like us, has to drag two sleds totalling more than double his body weight.

We managed to cover only a single mile (2 km). We planted our first signal flag, but felt no sense of accomplishment. We were exhausted; we couldn't hope to pull both sleds at once under these conditions. Richard racked his brains for ways to lighten the load, but found no solution; we were already down to the bare necessities. We will obviously have to revert to a shuttle technique, taking only one sled at a time. But this will slow our pace by half; it will take thirty days, not fourteen, to go forward the ninety miles (167 km) and establish the depot. Worse yet, the temperature dropped to −48°C (−54°F) as we made our camp. Although we'd put on every article of clothing we had, and had been struggling hard all day, we were chilled to the bone when evening came. We pitched the tent, and warmed the icicles that were our toes directly over the camp stoves.

FEBRUARY 15 (DAY TWO). We continued to struggle through the pressure ridges. Misha climbed one to gaze at what awaited us. A dispiriting and absolutely identical vista lay ahead. We dropped the sleds and began to scout in all directions, searching for a pathway through this hummocky nightmare. For three hours, we made no forward progress at all. We'd begun to lose hope when we came upon a gigantic block of ice that looked as if it had shattered into fragments the previous summer. But by slowly and painfully manoeuvring among its broken pieces, we could discern a path. It took us only thirty minutes to ski back to our sleds, but four solid hours to bring them up the trail. They sank into the soft, clinging snow. Darkness began to fall. We could go no farther; we felt as if we'd been crossing a white marsh that threatened to suck us in. We'd done everything we could, but our GPS reading confirmed that we'd covered only 0.7 miles (1.3 km) all day long.

Well, it's always easier to conceive a plan that to carry it out. We believed that we'd thought through every detail, foreseen every possible pitfall and stumbling block. But human powers have their limit, and this patch of ice had taxed us to the utmost. We could continue to pull the sleds, but only at this snail's pace. It is impossible to move more quickly if the ice doesn't change for the better, and there is no improvement in sight. This is as bad as the five-day delay imposed by the snowstorm in 1992! The horrifying possibility exists that we might fall so far behind schedule that the expedition will be doomed almost before it has begun.

FEBRUARY 16 (DAY THREE). Not content with throwing physical barriers in our path, the Arctic decided to hex our technology. We were forced to abandon the HEALTHSAT system, which had been malfunctioning from the outset. Several days ago, our receiver began to display outdated messages – ones we'd seen before, even though transmissions were supposed to be erased after five days. The satellite informed us that we were being sent new messages, but all we could receive were fragments. This left us in doubt as to whether our own new messages were reaching the recipients. So the HEALTHSAT fell by the wayside, along with its batteries. We left a little pile of flawed electronic wizardry beside the trail, right where we planted our third flag. We shall collect it again when we return. The only consolation is that our load has become marginally lighter, because we also left excess lunch food that we couldn't eat during the previous three days. (We mean that literally — we couldn't manage to swallow it. There was just too much; even though we were working terribly hard, our bodies weren't yet ready for the full 7,000-calorie-a-day diet.)

Actually, the constant or intuitive wish to shed unwanted weight sometimes takes an odd turn. Today, while we took a break, Misha was closing his backpack when a stick of butter dropped onto the snow. He decided to leave it there, and built a little marker — a sort of snow cairn — in the middle of the trail, in the rather remote hope that we'd stumble across it on the way back. We will try to follow our ski track when we return, and the marks of our sleds at least will still be visible (fresh snow is rather scarce at this time of year) — but the odds of finding a lonely shard of frozen butter are infinitesimal.

And trailside offerings are the least of our worries. We are plagued by minor mishaps, most of them attributable to the extreme cold. Everything becomes so brittle that it shatters if you look at it the wrong way. Misha snapped the binding on one of his skis, the tungsten tips of several ski poles broke off (thus rendering them useless on an icy surface), and the rubber inner portion of a stove's fuel line burst. The buckles on the straps holding the tops and bottoms of our sleds together came apart — but that was because they proved on close inspection to be slightly mismatched. Richard, the designated chief mechanic and jack of all trades, busied himself during rest stops trying to patch up all these faulty odds and ends. He even managed to fix our thermometer, which, after its last accurate reading of −40°C (−40°F), had developed air bubbles and couldn't be trusted.

We'd managed to make only another 0.5 miles (1 km), and fell into gloomy debate. First we counted our blessings: nothing really bad had befallen us; we were safe and sound, well fed and reasonably well rested, the ice was hard to deal with, but things could be worse, and so on. Well, they could perhaps be worse, but they could surely be better. One way or the other, we have to pick up the pace.

FEBRUARY 17 (DAY FOUR). Today we made slightly better time, and covered 1.3 miles (2.4 km) during seven hours. The light is pleasant while it lasts, casting a reddish-pink glow on the horizon. But the moon is little help; it sets after only two hours.

During one of the marches, Misha pointed out that we were spending far too long in scouting out our route. He suggested that, the next day, we adopt a different plan. "We cannot continue like this," he said. "We're making only a mile [2 km] a day, sometimes less. Let's leave the sleds wherever we make camp tonight. Then we'll take perhaps twenty kilograms [44 lb.] of food each, and go forward with just our packs, covering as much distance as we can. With luck, we can manage six, eight, or even ten miles [11, 15, or 19 km]. We'll leave the food wherever we get to – a sort of mini-depot. Then we can ski back for the sleds and pull them up along a freshly made trail. It doesn't matter if we only take one at a time. At least we'll have broken a trail and planted the flags. Anything is better than what we're doing now." Richard agreed, but with some misgivings. Being separated from the sleds, if only for a day, was an unsettling prospect. On our way back, we'd be skiing in the dark, with only our headlamps to guide us. Suppose a storm obliterated the trail. We wouldn't be able to find the marker flags; our GPS unit would freeze solid if we kept taking it out to navigate by; and we'd be forced to bivouac on the ice in −42°C (−44°F). But Misha was quite right. Potential perils couldn't be too much worse than the unproductive, draining drudgery that we'd faced during the last few days.

Another Arctic night. The moon refuses to show her face, blurring everything in total darkness. At such moments, a feeling of utter loneliness overwhelms your heart. You no longer think of yourself as travelling on the surface of planet earth; it's as if you've been transported to some alien galaxy. Somewhere in the depths of the universe there must be a small blue globe inhabited by humans like yourself; this is what you fix in your mind and strive to reach. But all around you is nothing but endless, oppressive, overwhelming darkness that drains your will and saps your ebbing strength.

FEBRUARY 19 (DAY SIX). Misha's plan is working. Yesterday we moved 6.5 miles (12 km) and left the contents of our packs at 83°18'. At four o'clock, we returned to camp; our headlamps worked well even in the pitch dark. The day was extremely clear; we could see all the way to Greenland in the east. A gorgeous sight; its mountain peaks were bathed in red.

Just before we turned back, we came to an ice river – a smaller version of the one that had very nearly finished us off in 1992. This one was older; it hadn't been active for quite a while. It had frozen solid, but its surface was the same grotesque jumble of smashed and broken floes interspersed with ditches and pressure ridges. It looked as if it would take us days to get across. In fact, it took us only an afternoon, because we found a narrow crack running through it that had frozen as well, offering a useful and relatively smooth pathway northward.

This evening, while getting ready to make supper, Misha climbed into the tent and asked Richard, who was still outside, to sweep the soles of his boots clear of snow. While trying to dangle his feet out through the flap, he brushed against a cooking pot full of water. This set off an Arctic chain reaction. Trying to save the pot, he upset another one, managed to steady it, but in doing so knocked into the first one again. Richard tried to lend a hand, but too late: the sleeping pads, the tent floor, and one of Richard's knees got nicely soaked. This delayed supper, which is the only thing we have to look forward to at the end of the day. Our lunches are certainly nothing to write home about. The double-smoked bacon has to be defrosted inside the tent and cut into tiny pieces for us to chew on as we ski along. Even if we keep them in our pockets, they harden into little bits of ice, and seem every bit as tasteless.

FEBRUARY 20 (DAY SEVEN). Our life is changing for the better. We covered four miles (7 km) today and seem to have moved past the area of extremely broken ice and soft snow that surrounds Ward Hunt.

FEBRUARY 21 (DAY EIGHT). Another 4.5 miles (8.3 km) during four and a half marches, for a total of seven and a half hours on the ice. Everything takes much longer than we'd anticipated. Even planting a flag so that it stands secure against the wind occupies us for five or ten minutes at a time; five flag-plantings add up to at least a march. Instead of standing there with a drill or ice auger, sinking bamboo poles, we should be moving towards our goal. At least the ice in this vicinity is reasonably stable and easy to move across, although the wind has created large, hard-packed drifts.

The sun is putting on a brief light show, painting the line where ice meets horizon a deep purple that softens gradually to pink. But the long night is in no rush to relinquish its hold. It's quite dark by 2 P.M., and we must use our headlamps after 5 P.M. in order to see a few metres in front of us.

Towards the end of the day, we reached a field of pressure ridges, but stopped short, not wishing to cross it in the dark. After we'd pitched the tent, Misha went outside and saw that the sky was full of stars, so bright that they seemed to cast a spell. He stood stock-still, his chin up, like a rabbit mesmerized by the stare of a snake. He wondered if he'd missed his calling in life. Perhaps, he thought, he should have been an astronomer. Perhaps so — but he was brought back to harsh reality when he noticed the first signs of frostbite on his fingers.

FEBRUARY 22 (DAY NINE). This morning the thermometer read −40°C (−40°F). Then it broke again, leaving us with only our frozen extremities to guide us until we returned to Ward Hunt, where we knew we could liberate another instrument from the hut.

We were sleeping warmly enough, although our bags were on the verge of icing up. Rolling and unrolling them in the morning and evening, we could hear and feel frost crystals crackle amid the down fill. Getting in and out of a sleeping bag is an exercise worthy of Houdini in his prime. If you aren't dead beat after skiing and pulling sleds all day long, you will be after you wrestle with the bag. Each evening we warmed the vapour-barrier liners — essentially, big plastic sacks — by keeping them folded up inside our clothes. The idea behind the liner is to block your perspiration before it reaches the bag. But you can't stop all of it; there's bound to be some condensation on the exterior of the liner, which will seep into the down baffles and freeze. (Pre-warming the liner helps to limit this effect, but only to some degree.) Frost is okay; it insulates, like snow. The trick is to keep it as frost. If it melts and freezes again, it will turn the down fill to little lumps of ice, and the bag will lose its power to insulate. It takes about half an hour just to get inside the bag. You're fully clothed, of course, including a fur hat. You zip the bag tightly, pull up a tubelike neckwarmer, and hope for the best. But all night long, your breath freezes and forms a halo of frost around your head. If you move, it falls on your face and wakes you up. Then it melts, and drips on you until you fall asleep again.

FEBRUARY 24 (DAY ELEVEN). We hadn't run into our old friend the Arctic white-out for quite some time, but today it decided to pay us a visit again. When it strikes, you feel as if you've fallen into a giant bowl of milk. You can see your hand in front of your face, but not much else. Marching in these conditions is obviously perilous; there's no telling what's underfoot, no warning of impending trouble.

But soon the weather cleared a bit, and we moved on, gaining another four miles (7 km) by the end of the day. In camp that night, we talked about the joys of returning, however briefly, to Ward Hunt. We looked forward to four wooden walls around us, a varied menu, and an assured supply of fuel. We were warm enough inside the tent — and would have stayed warmer if we could have slept standing up. Hot air rises, and the temperature near the roof was probably 20°C (68°F). But the floor remained well below zero. The fragile walls exhaled whatever heat accumulated within. During dinner, we sat close to the stoves, turning first one side of our bodies, then the other. Frost formed on our backs. Even our toothpaste froze solid, and we had to thaw the tube by holding it over a stove as we prepared our breakfast.

Under these circumstances, a tumble-down hut begins to look like a five-star hotel. We talk about the foods we'd enjoy when we touch base back at the island — engaging in a sort of Arctic psychotherapy session. Anything that reminds us of civilization brings diversity to our numbing routine. Even while we sleep, our minds are filling in the blanks in our existence. Richard finds that he is constantly experiencing peculiar dreams. Once, he sat through an entire gangster movie (although he didn't play a role). Often he finds himself in the middle of wild, erratic plot-lines and vivid, almost unnaturally bright colours. This is a natural reaction to what amounts to sensory deprivation. The brain resists the all-pervasive grey that shrouds the day, and recharges at night by taking refuge in brilliant fantasies.

FEBRUARY 25 (DAY TWELVE). A bitterly cold day, with a strong
southwest wind. Nothing can be handled with impunity; plastic
bindings become like pieces of hardened metal. If you touch
them with your bare hands, you'll wind up like a little kid with his
tongue stuck to a railing. The fingertips begin to turn white in
less than twenty seconds — as we learned while zipping up each
other's outer jackets (which you can't do for yourself, if you're
wearing thick mitts).

Misha fell victim to a frostbite attack from the rear. The wind
was at his back, but he was safe and secure inside his hood. Or so
he thought. When he stopped to check our position with the
compass, its built-in mirror revealed his face — a snow-white
plaster cast that looked like a death mask. Soon he felt as if
hundreds of ice needles were penetrating his body. Everything
around us seems drained by the cold, lifeless and unfamiliar.
Nothing functions as it should; the thermometer has long since
broken, but Richard discovered a novel way to keep track of the
temperature. If nothing else, the Weber–Malakhov expedition
has proved beyond doubt that a stick of butter changes consistency as the temperature drops. At $-35°C$ ($-31°F$), you can gnaw
on it. At $-40°C$ ($-40°F$), it snaps off cleanly, but at $-50°C$
($-58°F$), it shatters like glass. This so aroused Misha's entrepre-
neurial instincts that he urged Richard to take out a patent on the
idea, although its broader application remains somewhat obscure.

FEBRUARY 26 (DAY THIRTEEN). Today the character of the ice
changed. We ran into fewer drifts and walked across flatter, larger
pans covered with hard-packed, wind-blown snow. We checked
the bathometric map and found that we'd reached the edge of the
continental shelf, where the ocean drops from 200 to 1,400 metres
(656 to 4,593 ft.) deep in the space of five miles (9 km).

FEBRUARY 27 (DAY FOURTEEN). Our sleeping bags have iced up to the point of uselessness. Amid intense cold, we skied farther north, then walked around a very large pan of flat ice. Our intention had been to set up the depot at 84°30', and we had only reached 83°50', but we decided to stop here. It seemed like a good place. We had only done forty-five miles (72 km) in the fourteen days we had allowed ourselves, but the character of the ice had improved, and we were unlikely to do any better by going farther. We set up the Televilt and Argos beacons, which we buried in the snow. Placing them beneath the surface, out of the wind, should prolong their batteries. We made an inventory of the goods we were leaving behind. Richard is still uneasy about leaving the depot on the drifting ice. It will take us almost two and half weeks to return to Ward Hunt, retrieve the rest of our supplies, and return to this position. Will the Televilt work after sitting for that length of time in such extreme temperatures? Will the Argos really give us an accurate fix on the depot's location? If the depot drifts only marginally to the east – as research suggests – will we be able to find it? A mere five miles (9 km) of drift translates as an entire day's march.

FEBRUARY 28 (DAY FIFTEEN). It took us twelve hours to do all the work necessary to set up the storage depot. It wasn't, of course, a structure of any kind; building materials are hard to come by in the Arctic. Its drifting away is one problem, but our foremost worry is the possibility that it will be looted – not by our fellow explorer MacKenzie but by marauding bears, who'd look upon it as a picnic sent from heaven. Richard set up a complex and rather elegant booby trap, designed to scare off any animal bold enough to come near. The trap consists of a cat's cradle of trip wires. If anything touches one of the sleds, it will set off a shotgun shell loaded with black powder. The noise would be deafening, and the bear (or so we hope) would retreat unharmed in search of easier and quieter pickings. The device is equipped with three charges, but what if a bear is persistent and keeps coming back? Well, that is in the hands of fate. No one has ever left their supplies on the drifting ice before, and a hundred different things can go wrong.

But they can't concern us. We set off southward in the afternoon, carrying not enough rations to get us back to Ward Hunt. We'd calculated that we could make it with three lunches, one supper, and four bottles of fuel – a bare minimum, but we banked on locating the mini-depots we'd left along the way, their positions carefully marked with signal flags. We marched quickly, covering twelve miles (22 km) in eight hours. We could see the mountain peaks of Ward Hunt ahead of us, like sentinels on watch. The weather was in our favour. At one point, a fiery column of light appeared above the horizon, which usually signals that a clear day will follow. We grew happy at the idea of seeing one another by daylight. That alone would make the marches lighter. As we marched, we found that all our flags had remained in place. Only one had been blown away, leaving a sad stick in the snow. Every step takes us closer to Ward Hunt – but farther away from our supplies, left drifting on the imponderable vastness of the ocean.

CHAPTER THIRTEEN

MARCH 1 (DAY SIXTEEN). The first day of spring, but devoid of sun. An emotionless sky was covered with grey clouds. Darkness fell even earlier than usual, and it was difficult to keep to our track, even with our headlamps on. Only the most subtle signs – a lump of snow out of place, the mark of a single ski pole – enabled us to follow it. Nevertheless, we managed to walk thirteen miles (24 km) and arrived at a mini-depot where we collected enough food for breakfast tomorrow.

MARCH 2 (DAY SEVENTEEN). We awoke at 4 A.M., eager to make the most of whatever light the day would bring. We began our first march at a latitude of 83°24' – still nineteen miles (35 km) from Ward Hunt. Its mountains grew steadily closer, then disappeared from sight in the lowering cloud. We lost our way from time to time, regaining the trail only thanks to the flags that stretched like a dotted line across a white paper sea.

Today we found that our flag-planting technique had left something to be desired. When we'd first set off northward, we'd planted them farther apart, not knowing whether we'd taken enough to last us. Now we often couldn't see the next one and had to keep following the remains of the trail, counting the moments until we caught a glimpse of its dark rectangle.

When we reached 83°15', the snow grew harder, and our two-week-old trail became less perceptible. Misha took the lead, and we walked without pause, banking largely on intuition, for two and a half hours. We felt that if we stopped, we wouldn't be able to pick up the trail again. But luck was with us, and at 83°11', we found our former camp.

We had flags to spare and started to plant them as we went along, filling in the missing links. This slowed us, and we rested for twenty minutes only, fearful of wasting time. Darkness fell, and we lost all sign of the trail. Well, that couldn't be helped. We had to forge ahead in what appeared to be a straight line, which meant that we often took the course of most resistance. In the dark we were unable to scout out an easier route by detouring to one side or the other. We wallowed along through knee-deep, sometimes chest-deep, snow. We were starting to tire; we'd been

on our feet for more than twelve hours. When we hit a line of
pressure ridges that in the daylight we'd have sought a way
around, we removed our skis and attempted to break on through.
The beams of our headlamps made the surroundings seem even
more fantastic and menacing. An ordinary pressure ridge –
daunting enough if we'd been able to see it with any degree of
clarity – became a haunt of ogres or trolls that peered from
hidden caves, waiting to drag us in.

Suddenly, by sheer chance, we hit our previous trail, and
followed it for a short distance. And then, amazingly, we found
ourselves at the very place that Misha had dropped his lonesome
stick of butter on our way north. There it was, safely cradled in
its mound of snow. But what the Arctic gives with one hand, it
takes away with the other – and five minutes later, we lost the
trail again.

We could, and perhaps should, have called a halt and camped
until dawn brought fresh counsel. But we didn't dare, because we
were down to only one portion of supper each and a single bottle
of fuel. Our sleeping bags were iced up to a dangerous degree and
were incapable of keeping us warm; the thought of camping
under these conditions when a cosy hut awaited us was too much
to contemplate. Primitive though it was, we could count at least
on dry bags and light from the wind generator, so we pressed on.

Minutes stretched into hours, and we began to question the
wisdom of our decision. What were we doing in this never-
ending nightmare? We were confused and disoriented; we might
have got turned around amid the pressure ridges. For all we knew,
we were walking parallel to the coast. Misha suggested that we
verify our position with the GPS. Scarcely had he said so than we
felt soft snow beneath our feet. We realized at once that we'd
stepped onto the ice shelf. But where on the ice shelf were we? We
rummaged in our packs and took out the GPS, but found to our
disgust that its batteries were almost dead. We switched batteries

with the cameras — a tedious exercise that resulted in frostbitten fingertips. But the reading showed that we were right on course, standing only a few hundred metres away from our starting point.

Richard took a deep breath, turned to Misha, and said, "I owe you pancakes."

But not immediately. It took us an age to drag ourselves across the ice shelf. By the time we neared the hut, we'd been going virtually non-stop for seventeen and a half hours. Despite our fond imaginings, the hut proved to be only marginally more comfortable than the open ice. Its interior temperature was −35°C (−31°F) — a scant ten degrees warmer than the air outside. The tension that had built up over our long march was slow to dissipate. We were too exhausted to sleep; we couldn't believe we'd reached safe haven. But so we had, and the first stage of our journey had come to a very successful completion.

MARCH 4 (DAY NINETEEN). A day of rest and recovery. We are thawing out, enjoying ourselves, and doing as little as possible. Richard kept his promise and whipped up sourdough pancakes with maple syrup. What bliss it was to sit at a table and eat from proper plates! We know that our respite will be all too brief; that in a matter of days we'll be off again. But now is the time to relax and gather strength for the trials to come.

MARCH 5 (DAY TWENTY). Today we embark on a round of medical tests. Misha's eagerness to take people's blood and submit them to every conceivable test was legend during the Polar Bridge expedition and has not lessened in the interim. With a small centrifuge, he processed blood samples provided by both of us. Misha works with a professor in Russia, studying changes in hormones due to cold and stress. We packaged up the blood and will leave it here, to be picked up in June.

MARCH 6 (DAY TWENTY-ONE). Over breakfast we once again
debated whether to set off across the pressure ridges. The
prospect gave us pause; neither of us had ever attempted to work
so hard in such cold weather. The morning temperature was
−55°C (−67°F). But, after an hour or so, we decided that we
could wait no longer. The weather might not improve; in any
case, we couldn't sit in the hut forever. As we were making our
final preparations, we looked outside again. The thermometer
had dropped another degree while we were packing.

At first, believe it or not, we were too warm; we'd put on every
article of clothing we could think of. Misha offered yet another
example from his inexhaustible stock of Russian sayings: "Steam
never makes your bones ache" − meaning that it's better to
languish with heat than to suffer from the frost. In fact, if we
overheated momentarily, all we had to do was stop skiing and
stand still. In less than a minute, the cold would reassert itself,
and we'd continue on our way.

It was a gorgeous day − clear, with high visibility. There was
pink ice in the distance. The sun, appearing for the first time
since we left Iqaluit, broke through from behind the mountains
of Ellesmere Island, relieving the monochromatic grey of the
frozen surface. At this time of year, it is possible for us to stare
directly into the sun without fear of damaging our eyes. We often
turned to look back at it as it gradually changed tint from yellow
to orange through purple and lilac.

Although beautiful, the day is dangerously cold, with the
temperature dropping further, to −57°C (−71°F). While skiing
this afternoon, Richard felt as if he were breathing through a
straw. If you breathe deeply − as, of course, you must, if you're
working hard − you risk damage to the upper respiratory tract.
Shallow breathing deprives the body of oxygen, and you go
nowhere. You can't sit down or stand still; you have to shuffle
from foot to foot, staying in perpetual motion like a shark.

Soon we reached the pack ice and walked a few hundred metres along our former trail. Ahead of us loomed a supremely unwelcome sight that snapped us instantly alert – a shroud of fog that could only signal an expanse of open water where there'd been none three days before.

The moon had grown in size, attracting the ocean like a magnet and creating the first of what we feared would be many new leads. We walked up to it and probed its freshly frozen surface with our ski poles. There was only an insubstantial skin of ice; we easily poked holes through it. Plainly, it would not bear our weight. We scouted along its length, but failed to find a crossing place. We decided to leave our partial load right where it was and return to Ward Hunt for the next instalment.

MARCH 7 (DAY TWENTY-TWO). The temperature fell to −58°C (−72°F) overnight, but we could not afford any further delay. On the way back, we collected the HEALTHSAT from its icy cache. We were curious to see what had become of the lead that blocked our passage yesterday. To our delight, it had frozen solid, and we crossed it with ease. We recovered the supplies that we'd left at its edge and pressed on with the one sled combined. We found our trail on the other side of the lead and covered almost twelve miles (22 km) in only five and a half hours. Three weeks earlier, when we'd first marched north, it had taken us four days to walk this same distance.

On our way back, we walked in the dark, but the moon was up, illuminating our trail. We hurried along, fearful that the lead would open up again and cut off our retreat. The temperature had risen to −52°C (−62°F). Our clothes were damp from hoarfrost and our boot liners were soaking wet. We perspired heavily, damp as racehorses in the final stretch. Fortunately, the lead had remained closed, and we crossed it once again – but our hectic pace had taken its toll. Misha saw strange circles flashing before his eyes and could not shake off the illusion until we reached the hut.

Misha was not alone in his imaginings. On our way back from the depot several days ago, Richard had first noticed a very odd phenomenon: there seemed to be a third person beside us as we skied along. The presence wasn't menacing; it wasn't as if someone was "watching us." On the contrary, the sensation was supportive and benign. Richard began to look forward to the periodic arrival of our phantom friend and would later have to stop himself from turning to speak to whomever, or whatever, it was.

Much later, an acquaintance told us that we'd been in good company in more ways than one, and showed us a copy of the poems of T. S. Elliot. In "The Waste Land" – fitting, since we definitely felt like hollow men from time to time – Elliot describes exactly this feeling:

> Who is the third who walks always beside you?
> When I count, there are only you and I together
> But when I look ahead up the white road
> There is always another one walking beside you
> Gliding wrapt in a brown mantle, hooded
> I do not know whether a man or a woman
> – But who is that on the other side of you?

Elliot, whose poetry was so convoluted that he had to resort to footnotes, went on to credit his source: the lines "were stimulated by the account of one of the Antarctic expeditions (I forget which, but I think one of Shackleton's): it was related that the party of explorers, at the extremity of their strength, had the constant delusion that there was one more member than could actually be counted." So it was with us; and our friend would reappear from time to time as we went along.

MARCH 8 (DAY TWENTY-THREE). Will Steger's expedition set off exactly nine years ago today, and it would have been fitting to make our real start as well. But we decided to stay on Ward Hunt, having pushed ourselves to the limit yesterday, labouring for ten hours in −58°C (−72°F)! The temperature has bounced back to −50°C (−58°F). Towards evening it became practically balmy, rising to −44°C (−47°F). This cheers us up; it seems almost certain that tomorrow we can leave the land behind.

By mid-afternoon we'd heard the sound of an approaching airplane. It was a charted Twin Otter, bringing Og MacKenzie, the mystery Britisher. More details of his solo trip had surfaced on the Arctic grapevine. His timetable is rumoured to be sixty days, one-way; he is, as we mentioned earlier, going to travel unsupported.

The plane taxied to a halt, and MacKenzie started to unload his gear. He'd brought with him two enormous fibreglass and Kevlar sleds. Each is ten feet (3 m) long and weighed (we were told by the crew) 200 kilograms (440 lb.). Linked together, they looked like an articulated city bus − or, perhaps, two very commodious coffins on runners. We can't imagine how he hopes to lug these behemoths over the broken ice.

We approached the plane and greeted the new arrivals. MacKenzie wore a full face-mask that revealed only his eyes. He was civil enough, but expressed no interest in either of us. Two other men accompanied him. They were unsociable and reticent, totally indifferent to our presence. We learned that they planned to base themselves in Resolute for the next two months, "just in case." Exactly what they meant by this remained unclear.

Then, without further delay, MacKenzie shook our hands and

marched bravely northward. We were incredulous; he hadn't asked a single question! After all, we'd just travelled the path that he himself would take. If we'd been in his place, we'd have quizzed him on every detail. But off he went, lugging his tremendous load, without even a backward glance.

Two hours later, he was still in view, moving slowly across the ice shelf in the distance. We saw that he'd begun to drag one sled at a time, but even this must have been a Herculean effort. Well, no matter. The important thing was that we ourselves would be following more or less in his footsteps the next day. That evening we tried but failed one last time to send a message via HEALTHSAT. It was up to its old tricks, replaying messages that should have been erased by subsequent transmissions, and would definitely have to be left behind at the hut. The good news is that the Argos beacon we'd left at the depot is up and running – and that its position corresponds with the depot's location as plotted by the GPS. This means that the depot wasn't drifting to any great extent, and that we can be confident of finding it roughly where we thought it ought to be.

Chapter Fourteen

MARCH 9 (DAY TWENTY-FOUR). We awoke to a temperature of −51°C (−60°F). Richard busied himself with our final breakfast on shore – a sumptuous mixture of bacon and macaroni and cheese. As we set off, we looked across the ice shelf, but MacKenzie was out of sight; he must have been making his way down the far slope.

As we began to march, the temperature dropped to −54°C (−65°F). Within ten minutes we caught sight of MacKenzie, struggling with his sleds. He'd made camp last night on top of the ice shelf, only a few hundred metres from a warm hut.

We decided to approach him and make another attempt at conversation. As we neared, he removed his mask, revealing a kindly, bearded face – which in only a couple of seconds began turning white, along with his ears. Now he seemed more eager to talk, even at risk of frostbite. Fortunately, he realized his mistake and covered up again. He said that he'd spent the night in relative comfort, but that he'd had difficulty in lighting his stove. Its pump had frozen, and he'd had to warm it inside his clothing. He seemed almost totally unprepared – a raw novice stranded in an environment that would not forgive the slightest lapse on his part. We talked briefly about what awaited him along his line of march, then pulled ahead of him and left him to whatever might await.

Five and a half hours later, we reached our first planned camp, right on schedule. We erected the tent, but found that it offered little protection against the temperature, which remained unchanged. Hoarfrost formed on every surface. Silently, we have each begun to question our decision to travel in such extreme cold.

MARCH 10 (DAY TWENTY-FIVE). Today we covered another four miles (7 km), almost exactly according to plan. If we maintain this speed, we'll reach the food depot in nine days – but whether we'll be able to keep up the pace remains in doubt. It was severely cold in the morning, and we spent almost five hours preparing to go outside, meanwhile burning more fuel than we'd anticipated. Richard had a headache, and Misha prepared breakfast, which gave him a headache in turn. The cold had drained us of resolve; we seriously considered the prospect of returning to Ward Hunt and waiting there until the weather improved. But then we collected ourselves, to the extent that Richard could make his habitual joke. He smiled wanly as he shouldered his pack and said, "Just another day at the office."

The first march was sheer torture; we walked as if in a dream. The shuttle marches to the depot had spoiled us. We'd fallen out of practice in dragging heavy loads. Now we had one, and the slightest obstacle made us grind to a halt. We couldn't remain in harness — we had to unhook it and pull the sleds one by one with our hands. Our replacement thermometer registered −52°C (−62°F), as low as it would go. In fact, it was almost certainly even colder. Gradually, as the day wore on, we regained our strength, finding an instinctive rhythm. Indeed, by evening, we'd forgotten about our ailments and devoured our meal with a great appetite.

MARCH 11 (DAY TWENTY-SIX). Our prayers were answered, and the temperature rose to −39°C (−38°F). As usual, we began our morning by creating a virtual snowstorm inside the tent. Each day, one of us would remain inside, pass out the sleeping bags and foam sleeping pads, then sweep the interior clear of accumulated hoarfrost with our toilet brush.

Today the effects of frostbite were plain to see. Richard's cheeks were in bad shape, especially the left, which was yellowed and encrusted. On the right side, the skin was scabbed over and flaking off. Misha's nose looked much the worse for wear. These unattractive features were the result of the northeast wind that had been buffeting us for several days. To make matters worse, our noses were running like miniature Niagaras. Misha honked dolefully into a handkerchief every other minute, but Richard soldiered on, paying no attention, with an icicle hanging down. What a sight! We must look more like shuffling, snuffling winos than heroes of the high Arctic. At least we kept to our plan, and succeeded in marching 5.1 miles (9.4 km) before we made camp again.

MARCH 12 (DAY TWENTY-SEVEN). Shortly after breaking camp today, we ran into open water. The nearest crack was perhaps two metres (7 ft.) wide; steam rose from its surface. Now we knew why a dense haze had enveloped our tent overnight. The temperature had risen by five degrees, and snow had fallen in the early morning hours, but over a very clearly defined area, because warm (−4°C or 25°F) water evaporating from the crack had met −45°C (−49°F) air. The effect would have been even more dramatic and widespread if the crack had been wider. This is why infrared satellite photos of the Arctic Ocean display very odd groupings of colours and tints that seem at first glance to have no logical explanation. It's only the water at work; even the tiniest crack will cause the temperature to jump in the immediate vicinity, and a bigger lead will do the same over a radius of several miles.

MARCH 14 (DAY TWENTY-NINE). A grey and gloomy day. We felt tense and expectant as we broke camp, and by the end of the fourth march, our premonitions proved true. Our way was blocked by several cracks, and the sound of drifting ice could be heard in the west. On the opposite side of one crack, we could see our former trail, marked by a signal flag. Obviously, the almost full moon was pulling the ocean and cracking its fragile skin.

MARCH 15 (DAY THIRTY). When we awoke, the tent was cosy and warmer than usual. We took our sleeping bags outside and left them in the sun for a few hours. To our surprise, the sun was warm enough to dry them a little. As a rule, this shouldn't be the case until early April, when the sun would remain much higher above the horizon.

We spent the morning talking about Reinhold Messner – the famous German mountain climber who'd succeeded in conquering all the planet's 8,000-metre (approx. 26,000-ft.) peaks. He'd been the first up Everest without benefit of oxygen. The land held no new challenges for him, so he'd turned his attention to more symbolic pinnacles. Last year, on his first attempt, he'd made an unsupported journey to the South Pole. Then, despite the fact that he'd never set foot on the drifting pack ice, he'd declared that he would cross the Arctic Ocean from Russia to Canada, accompanied only by his brother Hubert, who also lacked experience in the North. They'd set off at about the same time as us; the fact that they'd chosen another route added a spirit of competition. Messner was surely a worthy rival, and we'd wondered from time to time how he was getting on.

Yesterday we found out. A message via TUBSAT told the story in stark though graphic terms: "Messner expedition over! Eleven miles only. Ice heaved, sled crushed. Hubert in H2O." In other words, poor Messner's adventure was over almost before it had begun. Fortunately, Hubert survived his ducking, and they were airlifted out by helicopter. We'd never have imagined that their attempt would come to such an untimely end – but it proved once again that the Arctic is a place apart, even for the boldest and most skilled explorer. We recalled the words of Hiroshi Onishi, who'd joined us on Icewalk (during which, by the way, the ice conditions were actually quite favourable). Onishi was also a skilled mountaineer; he, too, had stood at the top of Everest. And yet, as he put it, "It's easier to climb up Everest ten times than to get to the North Pole once." Alas, for Onishi will not climb again. He died in 1992 while attempting to conquer yet another mountain peak.

In any case, Messner was no longer in the running – and we had problems of our own. During the third march, we again heard the distant rumble of breaking ice. Then, immediately in front of us, two pans collided and a pressure ridge began to rear its head. We watched it as it was thrust skywards, displacing one of our flags. We turned left around it, because to the right an ominous expanse of "water sky" eroded the horizon – a sure sign that in that direction lay a fairly wide lead.

The ice vibrated beneath our feet, and more pressure ridges began to buckle up in front of us. We felt like tiny insects on a giant's palm, caught in the tightening grip of some unearthly power that crumpled and crushed the ice around us at every turn.

The worst of the movement subsided momentarily, and we began to edge our way along the pressure ridges. By doing this, we lost our former trail, but we hoped that we could reach the flag, check its number (and thus its coordinates), and use that information to get back on track. But this proved impossible. The flag was in the middle of a battlefield. Huge blocks of ice were breaking up all around it, and we had to continue scouting along the ridges to either side. In about 300 metres (984 ft.), we could make out the trail and follow it to a point from which we could see not one but three flags ahead. Frankly, the signal flags were getting on our nerves. They were like policemen: when we really needed one – say, in the midst of a white-out – they were nowhere in sight. When we had at least a semblance of a trail to follow, there they were, stretching off into the middle distance.

By now we'd reached a latitude of 83°42'. That evening, we camped beside one of the flags, checked its coordinates, and found that it had moved 1.5 miles (2.8 km) eastward since we'd planted it only weeks before. We had the moon to thank for this inexorable drift. Its pale yellow face hovered above us, ever on the watch. Misha now loathes its presence and says that he wishes he could banish it with the push of a button. (Neither of us has ever been able to overcome this animosity. Even now we can't bare to look at the night sky without suppressing the urge to shake our fists at our Arctic adversary.)

MARCH 16 (DAY THIRTY-ONE). We'd estimated that we should be able to reach the storage depot today in seven one-hour marches. After the first two, Richard felt suddenly weak and tired, but rebounded after lunch. Still, Misha's pace proved too rapid for him, and he lagged slightly behind, although moving well at his own speed.

After our final rest period, a huge lead measuring at least 120 metres (394 ft.) wide stretched diagonally across our path. But a skin of more-or-less stable ice had formed, and we crossed it without major difficulty. A smoky blue haze filled the air, alerting us to the possibility that even more open water lay ahead. And so it did. We noticed an abrupt change in the consistency of the snow, and clouds of steam arising from the ice. Misha was the first to mount one of the pressure ridges and see what awaited us. When Richard caught up with him, he stood silently, unable to utter a word.

Blocking our path was one of the widest leads we'd ever seen. It was dusk, and we couldn't make out the far shore.

"Richard," Misha said, "believe it or not, but that lead is really large." "You're kidding," Richard replied; and we stood in silence for a moment longer, trying to reason our way out of a seemingly impossible situation.

Assuming that our depot was not already lying on the bottom of the ocean, there, somewhere on the opposite side of the lead, were half our provisions – including an inflatable boat that would have enabled us to cross. What could we do to reach them? We scouted eastward, but with disappointing results. The ice surface was mottled with cracks. Some were covered with young ice, but it was too thin to walk on. We feared that this would be the case if and when we crossed over to the depot; perhaps the pan it rested on had been weakened as well. We searched for two- or three-day-old ice that would bear our weight, but to no avail. We walked back, ate some chocolate, and reconnoitred to the west. Nothing but open water met our eyes, zigzagging away out of sight.

This time it was Richard who voiced an apt Russian proverb: "Morning is wiser than evening." That remained to be seen, but at the moment, there was nothing to be done, and we were forced to make camp where we stood. As we did so, the full moon – a huge bright-orange ball – rose to mock us once more. "You miserable insects," it seemed to say, "what made you think you could reach your depot with no problems?"

Lying in our sleeping bags, we tried to derive what scant comfort we could from our predicament. The ice is moving, and moving earlier than we'd expected. Fine; that's the fault of the trickster moon, and is beyond our control. The good news is that as far as we can determine, we are in the middle of a very large ice field, known as a massif. It is cracking, but it is also shifting as one enormous body – the component pieces aren't breaking away and sailing off in all directions. That's why we'd managed to follow our trail with some measure of success. That's why we expect the depot to be where it should be, not drifting free. All we have to do is cross the lead tomorrow morning and we'll be reunited with our supplies.

MARCH 17 (DAY THIRTY-TWO). When we awoke, Misha climbed a pressure ridge to see what if anything had happened during the night. He thought he could see a signal flag about 700 metres (2,300 ft.) to the northwest. At least we hadn't drifted far during the night. Indeed, now that the full moon was past, the ocean's movements should decrease. The lead has begun to close up and freeze over, but its movement remains volatile – pressure ridges had sprung up nearby. It might open again at any moment, and we had to make haste.

There was no time for a preliminary reconnaissance; we set off immediately across the frozen surface of the lead. But with only 100 metres (328 ft.) to go, the surface turned to open water again. We veered left and found a crossing place. At last we reached the edge of the pan that supported the depot. There were our sleds, waiting patiently by the final signal flag. They were perfectly intact – not even a fox had come calling, let alone a bear. Now we could rest easily at nights, untroubled by dreams of our supplies plummeting to the ocean floor. We threw our sleeping mats onto the ice and sat watching the sun slope downward through the sky, closer and closer to the far horizon.

CHAPTER FIFTEEN

MARCH 18 (DAY THIRTY-THREE). Today we rested, having spent thirteen hours in our sleeping bags. We had to prepare ourselves for even more strenuous efforts in the days to come. Now that all our supplies were together again, our loads would become much heavier. To manage them, we'd have to adopt more flexible tactics. On smooth, even ice, we could drag both sleds at once, but if the going got rough, we would take them one at a time. We packed the four sleds with seventy-two days' worth of food, the same amount we carried after Bob Mantell departed from us in 1992. Their total weight is back up to 140 kilograms (309 lb.), plus twenty kilograms (44 lb.) in our packs.

We can't predict whether the Arctic spring will arrive earlier than usual this year. The signs are ominous: the lead we'd just succeeded in crossing keeps stirring all night long. It makes a low, ominous grumble, rather like a construction project taking place in the distance. There is a dull, throbbing *chuk-chuk-chuk* – then, when a piece of ice falls, a louder, sharper *bang*.

We boiled a pot of water and began to repair our physical appearance. Richard's frostbitten cheeks are recovering, but the bridge of his nose remains heavily scabbed. Misha found a bar of soap, Richard produced an unused razor blade, and we enjoyed a shave, growing younger-looking with every stroke. Now we are ready for fresh adventures.

MARCH 19 (DAY THIRTY-FOUR). We began by pulling only one sled each, because of rough ice. Later, when the surface evened out, we linked both sleds together. Misha set a brisk pace, but Richard was having trouble. The slightest bump or ripple impeded him, and a twenty-centimetre (8-in.) snowdrift became a major stumbling block. Still, we gained 2.9 miles (5.4 km) and found that during the previous night we'd drifted an additional 200 metres (656 ft.). Every little bit counts — as does the fact that, each day, the food we eat and the fuel we burn reduces our total weight by 1.5 kilograms (3.3 lb.) each.

MARCH 20 (DAY THIRTY-FIVE). We covered another 4.3 miles (7.9 km) towards the Pole and drifted very slightly in the right direction. But we are uneasy about accepting this sort of free ride from the ocean currents. The Arctic is capricious; the drift might turn against us at any time. Today the ice resembles the conditions on the Russian side — large pans punctuated only by distinct pressure ridges, with fewer randomly broken areas in between.

During the second march, however, we hit a very volatile stretch of young ice that suddenly cracked and opened immediately in front of us. We scouted in opposite directions, looking for a place to cross. The ice grumbled sullenly beneath our feet. Steam rose into the leaden sky. We felt as if we were boiling in a huge pot — polar missionaries about to be consumed by cannibals — the difference being that our pot was freezing cold.

Perhaps in keeping with the idea of someone making someone else's meal, Richard came to an abrupt stop. "Are you hungry?" he asked. Misha was at a loss to fathom the question, but answered, "Not yet." "Too bad," said Richard. "Look! There's a seal in the water." And so there was, bobbing up and down in the lead, and curiously craning his neck to catch a glimpse of the interlopers on his turf. We had plenty of food, so we didn't bother to unpack the gun. The seal watched us as we found a crossing place and ferried the sleds across on a makeshift bridge composed of floating blocks of ice.

Just then one of Misha's sleds sloped sideways into the water. He hauled it out immediately, but it emerged with a slick coating of ice – an additional and very unwelcome weight.

Fortunately, we hit an excellent patch of ice and made good time over four more marches. We managed to pull both sleds at once, slowed down only by the occasional drift. Richard had by now recovered his strength. The previous day, moving across flat pans, he could scarcely move his load, but today Misha barely maintained the lead, although he was able, as usual, to better pull his sleds through heavy snow, up pressure ridges, and over drifts. The weather cooperated as well, and we made 4.2 miles (7.7 km), aided by a southwest wind. Sometimes Misha would stop and ask Richard's opinion of the route, careful always to avoid ill-feeling and keep the inevitable friction to a minimum.

Towards evening the temperature rose to − 29 °C (− 20 °F), and when we turned in, the tent's interior was almost hot. It seems as if the calendar has skipped the better part of a month; all this is far more typical of mid- to late April.

MARCH 22 (DAY THIRTY-SEVEN). We started at noon and went on until half past eight in the evening, gaining 2.7 miles (4.9 km). At one point, we hit a large, flat pan, absolutely free of drifted snow, that might have served as a landing strip. More often, though, we were slowed by zones of badly broken ice that forced us to remove our skis and clamber over numberless pressure ridges. Shuttle marches were the order of the day. At least the sun was up and shining brightly. We stopped for a rest, sat down on our sleds, and enjoyed a snack with our back turned to its warm rays like two basking polar bears.

Just before making camp for the night, we crossed a narrow crack, covered with fresh, young ice, which seemed to stretch northward for a considerable distance. We talked about using it as a convenient pathway the following day – but the Arctic must have eavesdropped on our conversation.

During the night, Misha had a peculiar dream. It was spring, and he was a young boy again, watching an ice-breaker make its way up the Oka River near Kusminskoye, the village where he was born. The air was filled with dazzling splashes of water; the crunch and crackle of the ice could be heard many kilometres away.

Suddenly, he found himself in a frigid Arctic tent, but the soundtrack of his dream remained loud and clear. Richard awoke as well. This was no dream; the ice was moving practically beneath our campsite. We huddled in our sleeping bags, listening to its rattle as it chewed up the crack that we wanted to use as tomorrow's route north.

This isn't the first time that something of this nature has occurred. It's enough to make us downright superstitious. The Arctic seems to be a living presence, with ears that overhear the hopes of puny travellers. Scarcely do you dare to wish for better conditions, voicing or even thinking about the possibility that your luck will change, than the world turns upside down, just to remind you that you represent only inconsequential grains in the Arctic mill – a mighty engine waiting for the chance to grind you down.

MARCH 23 (DAY THIRTY-EIGHT). Today we came upon large pans of flat, young ice, no more than a year old and strangely blue in colour. We made several marches, but there seemed to be no end to them. When we stopped for the night, Misha complained

that we had nowhere to pitch our tent: there wasn't enough snow
to weigh down its bottom edges, not enough even to scoop up a
handful to melt for drinking water. Nor was it reassuring to camp
on such a recently formed surface. If the ice began to move again,
our pan would be the first thing to crack. Just imagine – short of
snow in the middle of the Arctic Ocean! Finally, we anchored the
tent as best we could, and scraped a little snow from the ice,
hoping that it would be fresh enough to drink when boiled. (You
can't, of course, drink melted surface ice; it's frozen salt water.)

MARCH 24 (DAY THIRTY-NINE). We reached a latitude of
84°12', having advanced twenty-two miles (41 km) in six days –
very significant progress, more than we could have expected or
hoped for. With the exception of Peary's expedition, no prece-
dents exist for what we're doing on the ice. No one has travelled
so far north so early in the year.

But during one of our breaks, Richard stated that he had no
wish to spend another March on the Arctic ice. "It's too cold, too
heavy," he said. "We're doing it, and that's fine. But I've done it
too many times and I don't want to do it again. The more I'm
away, the more I miss Josée and the kids. The longer you live with
someone, the more they become a part of you – and the more you
miss them when they aren't there." Misha wasn't totally surprised,
but replied that "one should never say never." "Nobody knows
what may happen in the future," he said. "Let's finish this expedition, and then we'll see what the future brings." But both of us are
feeling fed up with the frozen wastes and are numbed by the
−39°C (−38°F) cold that goes on, day after weary day.

Tonight we talked about our predecessors and the expeditions
that they'd mounted in the early part of the century. What had
contributed to their failure? Roald Amundsen, for example, had
attempted to reach the Pole by means of a plan originally devised

by Fridtjof Nansen: the idea was to allow his ship, the *Maud*, to get locked in the ice somewhere near Chukotka, then simply drift across towards Greenland, passing near the Pole en route. We believe that Amundsen hoped that by doing so he would be recognized as the first to reach the Pole; he did not believe that Robert Peary had made it. But Amundsen made a mistake, and sent two men to their deaths. His crew had wintered off the Taimyr Peninsula in 1919. In the fall, he dispatched two of them — Tessem and Knudsen — on a journey overland from Cape Chelyuskina to Dikson, a distance of 1,000 kilometres (621 mi.). Worse yet, they departed at the onset of the polar night. The odds were against them, and they perished in the darkness. Knudsen's remains were never found, but Tessem's were located. He had died within sight of Dikson. A memorial plaque in that town bears his name, and we had seen it before embarking on the 1988 Polar Bridge expedition. Misha had once been part of a group that attempted to retrace the route of the doomed explorers; and Richard, intrigued by the story, had remembered it when he and Josée were about to name their first-born son (although they put a slight twist on the spelling, changing the second "e" in Tessem to "u").

Why was Amundsen's expedition marked by tragedy? Why had he sent those two men off to almost certain death? Was his team plagued by psychological problems and clashes of personality — the pitfalls that we were at pains to avoid at any cost? To be sure, we went through many a difficult moment — but we were two equals, complementing, not competing with, one another. Neither of us has ever wished for a moment that he were travelling with another partner.

MARCH 26 (DAY FORTY-ONE). The band of flat, young ice swung off to the east, and we proceeded onto old ice again — hard slogging as usual. Towards evening the temperature dropped to

−48°C (−54°F). During the last march, Misha felt as if someone were sticking a needle into his cheek. He touched it with his hand; he might as well have been stroking a piece of wood. The flesh was white and icy cold; very shortly, another layer of skin crusted over and fell off.

MARCH 27 (DAY FORTY-TWO). A dispiriting day, filled with minor mishaps. It started badly, with a temperature of −40°C (−40°F). Our bags were icy cold, and Richard had found it difficult to fall asleep. He was drained of energy, able only to put one foot in front of the other, running on sheer will power and survival instincts. As the day wore on, the temperature rose to −22°C (−8°F) in the sun, but in the evening, we ran afoul of our stoves. We'd fallen into the habit of burning two (of a total of three) simultaneously at full power for ten minutes at a time to heat the tent and dry our gear. Now two of them developed leaks and blockages, and the temperature inside the tent dropped to −38°C (−36°F).

MARCH 30 (DAY FORTY-FIVE). A day of rest and a change in diet: Lipton soup and raspberry crystal drink. Richard succeeded in fixing both stoves. And just as well — it's terrible to think about what would happen if we were reduced to a single heat source. We darned our boots where the ski bindings had rubbed them down and indulged in another shave. A good housekeeping tip: nylon boots can be mended with needle and dental floss instead of thread. In the Arctic, you'd better be able to piece things together when the need arises. Some people don't have the knack: during one of his expeditions, Ranulph Fiennes threw away his skis because the bindings snapped. The Inuit are role models in this regard. Once, we met a native hunter who had been stranded on Baffin Island, 300 kilometres (186 mi.) from the nearest town. His snowmobile had broken down, and he needed to drill a hole through a metal plate in order to make the repair. But he had had no drill — so he took out his gun and shot a hole in the plate.

Meanwhile, in the outside world, things are going well. Deb Hine has been faxing weekly updates to our sponsors and is about to send out the third expedition newsletter. It's good for us to reflect on the fact that we aren't alone: our team is doing great work on our behalf. Tim Kenny is on top of every detail, Josée has been sending us encouraging and timely messages: "Hot outside; tomorrow will not wear snowsuit or mitts, love Tessum. Keep spirits high & attack; See you in June, Ward Hunt Island, Josée & Olga." Michel Perron acts as a tower of strength in the background. The Follow Us students are in almost daily contact, and Deb reports that media coverage has been steady and positive, thanks to Peter and Tom Mateuzels. What a change from our experiences in 1992, when most of our support team was telling us to get off the ice!

MARCH 31 (DAY FORTY-SIX). Today was beautiful — sunny and clear, with a feeling of spring in the air. Soon other expeditions will be swarming around the Pole. We learned today that Will Steger, who was attempting a supported crossing of the Arctic Ocean, is stuck on Sredny, waiting to be helicoptered north so as to make a start from 85°. We know what he and his party are going through. The island's amenities are ghastly: a collection of crude huts filled with acrid cigarette smoke and a single television with an eerie green screen that plays awful Russian programs.

We also learned that Og MacKenzie has been having a terrible time. At last count, he'd covered only seven miles (13 km) from Ward Hunt. How will he manage to pull his mammoth sleds in $-50°C$ ($-58°F$) temperatures? We have no idea why he persists in remaining on the ice. (He didn't for very long. He was picked up a week or so later, and disappeared from view.)

APRIL 1 (DAY FORTY-SEVEN). No sooner had we congratulated ourselves on having survived March than a snowstorm struck and continued for two full days and nights. We pulled our sleds through soft, puffy snow the consistency of cotton wool. Visibility was poor, and it was difficult to select a path. We plunged straight ahead, stumbling into unseen drifts. We'd stop, turn back, and pull the sleds by hand. Our skis would sink, and we'd have to take them off and proceed on foot. We felt as if we were going nowhere, marching on a treadmill. In fact, we made a mere 4.4 miles (8.1 km), and reached a latitude of 84°46'. But the storm had blown in warmer temperatures. When we made camp, it was only −15°C (5°F) outside and −6°C (21°F) inside the tent. We seemed to have entered a sort of anticyclone, or low-pressure zone. The usual reading this time of year should be more like −30°C (−22°F).

APRIL 2 (DAY FORTY-EIGHT). Today was hell — a brute survival day. We slogged through fresh snow that lay half a metre (2 ft.) deep. To make matters worse, the ice was rough beneath it. We made only 4.1 miles (7.6 km), and both of us were in foul moods. Richard said, "I want to be home at 151 Basswood. In these conditions, with all this weight, it's too much for me. I can't go on like this; tomorrow we have to change our plan." For Richard, it was the low point of the entire expedition. Misha said, "I'd like to be home, too, but this is where we are." We are banging our heads against the wall. All of the omens are bad: we've encountered May weather a month early; and who knows what that might foretell? We'll have to conserve our energy; there is no point in half-killing ourselves over eight marches if we cover less than five miles (9 km) a day.

APRIL 3 (DAY FORTY-NINE). The full moon, our old nemesis, is coming back to haunt us. We don't have to look skyward to

February 12, 1995. A technician prepares to throw a parachute flare to light up the ice at Ward Hunt Island, enabling the First Air Twin Otter to land. The flare burns at 1.5 million candlepower; half a mile away one can read a newspaper by its light.

During our rest period at Ward Hunt, after setting up the depot, Misha processes blood samples we have both provided. With a professor in Russia, he is studying changes in hormones due to cold and stress.

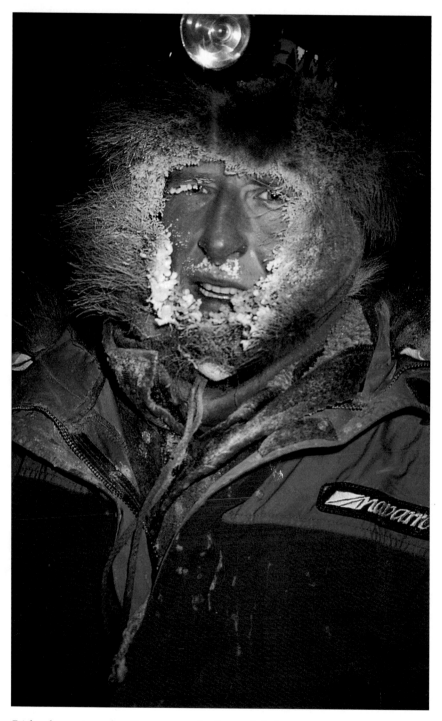

Richard, wearing a headlamp to see in the total darkness.

Leaving Ward Hunt Island on March 9 to begin the main expedition after setting up our depot. This is the first sun since leaving Iqaluit; the temperature is -54°C (-65°F).

Skiing around a lead.

Misha, emerging from our tent.

Confirming our arrival at the North Pole. The location is legible; accuracy ± 100 metres.

Misha

Misha enjoying boiled seal ribs. Ours was the first North Pole expedition to hunt successfully; for some reason, Peary's Inuit failed to find seals.

One of two leads we cross using our 1.5-kg Russian inflatable boat.

The last big ice wall that separates ocean ice from shore ice. We had met it in February, on our way north, and had named it the Great Wall of China. As we climbed it now, we were grateful we had already dumped the sleds and all other equipment that was no longer essential.

Just before stepping onto land, June 14, 1995.

verify that it is growing in size – that fact is evident in the ever-widening cracks that impede our path. It is hard to detect them, lurking beneath the freshly fallen snow. The surface might appear solid enough, but if we probe with our ski poles, they go right through. We don't want to follow them, down into the abyss – the ocean here is at least 1,600 metres (5300 ft.) deep.

This evening we discussed our situation and decided to make fewer marches each day. We'll lose ground, but we can gain it back when conditions improve. Meanwhile, we can conserve our lunch foods to some degree. We'll lag behind our plan, but that was only an approximate schedule that looked good on paper. Also, we agreed to switch positions in the middle of the march, rather than at the end, so that each of us would spend less time leading the way through unbroken snow without a break. Besides, visibility is down to practically zero; no one is going anywhere fast. As we turned in for the night, we could feel the frozen lumps of down inside our sleeping bags. In the morning, they'd defrosted, but that meant only that we were warming the bags, instead of them warming us.

APRIL 4-5 (DAY FIFTY). The sun reappeared from time to time, although the snow remained soft and treacherous. Nonetheless, our tactics worked, and we managed to cover an additional 6.2 miles (11.5 km), equalling the record pace we'd set when conditions were close to ideal. More importantly, we succeeded in crossing 85° – the magic number that strengthens the resolve of every polar expedition. We were certainly doing better than our competitors. We received a message via TUBSAT that Mitsuro Oba, who was attempting to reach Canada via the Pole from Russia, had been evacuated due to severe frostbite. Another rival out of the running; it seems to be an unlucky year, and we hope that we will prove to be the exception to the rule.

APRIL 5-6 (DAY FIFTY-ONE). A white haze hung above us for much of the day, but cleared towards evening, when the sun peeked briefly through. We crossed a lead that widened to form what looked like an octagonal lake, cut in half by a narrow strip of pressure ridges, rather like a dam or levee. In a few days, the moon will be full, and we can expect a great deal more open water of all descriptions in our path.

Early in the day, Misha had remarked that at least there probably weren't any bears within a 100-kilometre (62-mi.) radius. He soon had occasion to reconsider his words. During our third march, we spotted huge (and very fresh) footprints in the snow. As we moved on, we kept anxiously looking back over our shoulders. It wouldn't be hard for the hungry beast to catch our scent. But what was it doing up here in the first place? There are few bears on the Arctic Ocean, for the excellent reason that they can't find enough to eat — unless, of course, you count a pair of prepackaged explorers. That night Richard jumped suddenly into the tent, shouting, "I am a huge white bear!" After which, just to be on the safe side, he carefully rechecked the rifle.

APRIL 6-7 (DAY FIFTY-TWO). Our "working day" has lengthened to twenty-six hours; we are quite literally moonlighting our way to the Pole. But the going was very hard through large expanses of badly broken ice. We gained only 4.7 miles (8.7 km); we needed a wind to blow away the snow. Instead, during our final march, the ice began to shake and shift beneath our feet. Ahead of us, clouds of steam obscured the horizon. A wide lead blocked our way, as if to repay us for commenting earlier in the day that the full moon hadn't yet produced its worst upheavals. We camped a short distance away from the open water, and the ice around our tent shifted ominously all night long.

APRIL 9-10 (DAY FIFTY-FIVE). Today we were forced to cross countless cracks and leads. On the rare occasions that we came to an expanse of relatively flat ice, a headwind would spring up and push us back against our harnesses. A snow squall completed this very depressing picture, and visibility dropped to nil.

From time to time, we followed leads that were skimmed with new ice, seven to ten centimetres (3 to 4 in.) thick. This was a pleasure, but only briefly. Thin ice is fragile, and the slightest drift distorts its crust, creating frozen waves.

Hard going for us! – but not for another seal, which peered at us from one of the leads, rising up to reveal almost half its sleek, black body. Curiosity had overcome its instinct for self-preservation. Should we shoot it to augment our diet? Our own self-preservation asserted itself. The flesh would burden our sleds with an additional ten or twelve kilograms (22 or 26 lb.), and we decided to wait until our supplies ran down.

That night the drift intensified, pushing us 1.9 miles (3.5 km) south and westward by almost half a degree of longitude – another 2.5 miles (4.6 km). Obviously, the Arctic has fresh tricks up its sleeve.

CHAPTER SIXTEEN

APRIL 11 (DAY FIFTY-SIX). A strong north-by-northeast wind was pushing us back the way we'd come. We'd drifted 2.5 miles (4.6 km) south overnight – more than half the distance we'd gained the previous day. If this keeps up, then every other working hour we'll drift 0.15 miles (0.27 km) south and westward 0.3 miles (0.6 km). Six miles (11 km) forward progress will be reduced to 4.5 miles (8.3 km). Then, during the nights, we'll drift again. So much effort, for so little return!

But even greater efforts will not avail. The ice opens up, thanks to the full moon; the drift is determined by the wind. The weather will not change to suit our purposes. We had never experienced such warm temperatures this early in the year. We had assumed that we'd encounter sunny conditions with a hard frost and stable readings of −25°C (−13°F) or −30°C (−22°F). But here we were, wandering around in a white haze, with a reading of only −13°C (9°F) in the morning, zero visibility, and fresh, crisp snow.

We had to summon up all our resolve and strive to make six marches daily, each an hour and ten minutes long. If we get back on schedule, we will be able to rest for twenty-four hours in two days' time. We have provisions for forty-seven days. If we reach the Pole in twenty-five days, that will leave us with sufficient food for a twenty-two-day return journey. Worse comes to worst, we can shoot a seal and restock the larder. But we cannot be delayed en route, and we'll have to cover ten to twelve miles (19 to 22 km) daily. This will be difficult, but not impossible. Soon we'll be able to switch to one sled each, having used up a fair proportion of our supplies. Day by day, the load is lessening as we consume our food and fuel.

Last night Misha had another dream. His wife, Olga, arrived in Canada with their sons and went to an unfamiliar hotel. He roamed the corridors looking for them, but failed to locate their room. We hope this does not symbolize our attempts to reach the Pole.

APRIL 12 (DAY FIFTY-SEVEN). Huge snowflakes fell from the sky, and we walked like figures in a black-and-white movie, disoriented by the gathering haze. The temperature rose to −8°C (18°F).

What was the matter with this wretched weather? Nonetheless, we managed to pick up the pace. Yesterday we covered 6.8 miles (12.6 km) – a record distance. The wind shifted to the northwest, then died down altogether. This cut our southward drift to only 0.5 miles (1 km) in ten hours.

In the morning, lying in our sleeping bags, we settled on a good description of our polar quest. It was like a tug-of-war – whenever we pulled harder, the Arctic pulled back, regaining ground and throwing us off balance. Today it treated us to everything in its rich and varied arsenal: zero visibility, rough ice, shifting floes, open water, and knee-deep, freshly fallen snow. The only weapon it held in reserve was a killing frost. A month ago, we'd struggled to endure $-58°C$ ($-72°F$). Now the thermometer read a full fifty degrees warmer. We bridged a crack by tossing snow onto a floating block of ice. The instant we'd crossed, it sank beneath the water. Fifteen minutes later, we hit another lead, and then another. By day's end, we'd made only 4.7 miles (8.7 km). We pitched camp at 85°33', and decided to rest there tomorrow.

APRIL 13 (DAY FIFTY-EIGHT). The Arctic rewarded us overnight, and we drifted very slightly to the north. Strangely, the southern wind also brought an influx of colder air, and the temperature dropped to $-22°C$ ($-8°F$). We made an inventory of our goods and repacked the remainder into one sled each, abandoning some spare clothing and other personal belongings. A flurry of good luck messages arrived via TUBSAT, including one from Borge Ousland and Sur Mordre in Norway. It's nice to know that people are cheering us on. (In a day or two, we'd receive yet another communication from Paul and Mette Lavelle, reading: "On Into History – Happy Easter.") We needed a boost, because we'd fallen fourteen miles (26 km) behind schedule. But even as we sat and recovered our strength, we drifted another 1.3 miles (2.4 km) closer to the Pole – an infinitesimal distance, but we'll take anything we can get.

APRIL 14 (DAY FIFTY-NINE). One sled each has made our lives much easier. We covered 9.8 miles (18.1 km) and drifted a further 0.7 miles (1.3 km) during the night – excellent progress.

Towards the end of the day, we saw a strange trail that we thought at first was the ski track of another expedition. But when we neared it, it proved to be the marks of a group of polar bears – probably a mother and her cubs – not the sort of visitors you'd wish to meet unawares.

In camp that night, we heard a strange noise – a rhythmic thumping that sounded like someone hammering. We went outside and saw open water quite nearby. The sound was its fragile coating of ice, snapping as it expanded and contracted.

APRIL 16-17 (DAY SIXTY-ONE). The wind shifted to the west, and we could no longer count on drifting towards the Pole while we slept. Instead, we'd been pushed back 0.5 miles (1 km), and our eastward drift had increased dramatically – a total of ten miles (19 km) during the previous day and night. To compensate for the eastward drift (to the right), we ski 15° to the left of the Pole. Fortunately, we'd been making good time, covering 1.4 miles (2.6 km) in a single march, but we'd also spent almost fourteen hours in motion. Misha fell asleep over dinner; he was too exhausted to feel hunger. Our mood wasn't blue, it was dull – dull as the sky, the haze, and everything else around us. The temperature had climbed back to −8°C (18°F). Could spring have arrived a month early? Even the smaller cracks will prove to be uncrossable if their surface doesn't freeze, but this demands an average high of −15°C (5°F).

APRIL 17-18 (DAY SIXTY-TWO). We continued to drift eastward, and it began to blow again, our fifth snowstorm since the end of March. Richard admitted that he was very tired, and Misha felt the same, although he was less inclined to speak of it out loud. Our backs and shoulders ache constantly, as we knew they would; pain is part of the bargain.

APRIL 19 (DAY SIXTY-THREE). The sun appeared, but the wind rose, robbing us of what ought to have been record progress. We made eight marches and felt certain that we'd covered at least twelve miles (22 km) – but when we checked our coordinates, we learned that we'd gained only 7.5 miles (13.8 km). The drift continued to frustrate all our efforts. We pitched camp on reliable-looking ice, in the lee of a pressure ridge – but when we began to light the stoves, the ridge began to shift, making so much noise that we couldn't tell whether the stoves were functioning. Then, without warning, the tent pole fell, knocking over a cooking pot full of noodles. The stove had been working all right and had melted the ice beneath the pole. We scraped up sticky pasta from the tent floor, as Misha kept muttering, "There goes all our energy for tomorrow."

APRIL 20-21 (DAY SIXTY-FOUR). This morning the wind dropped, the drift slowed, and the thermometer registered −22°C (−8°F). Skiing became almost enjoyable for the first time in what seemed like ages. We made eight marches, seventy-five minutes each, and then looked for a place to camp. Our rule was always never to rest or stop on the wrong side of a lead or else the Arctic was bound to make it more difficult to cross. This time, however, there were so many stretches of open water that we gave up and pitched our tent.

It's funny being out here on the ice. Everything normal is in limbo or on hold. Our routine is our only reference point; there's no other reason to keep track of the passage of time. There are no days, no weeks; the date doesn't really matter. The sun goes round and round. There's no real difference between night and day. Everyone else who matters – your family, your friends – is so far away, so unreachable. We receive odd little messages on the TUBSAT – abbreviated scraps of information that verge on trivia. The messages let us know that people are thinking about us, just as we're thinking about them, but it's not communication in any real sense, only a form of encouragement at a distance. We ski eight marches, sleep, and eat. Then we make another eight marches, and so forever on. If it's a nice day, it's nice. If it isn't nice, it's awful. Our entire universe is bounded by the Arctic and the task at hand.

This morning, for example, we received a message from Tom Mateuzels, asking on behalf of the media how we felt and what we missed the most. Misha's answers were: strong; and friends, doughnuts, and a warm washroom, in that order. Richard said that he felt strong in the morning, tired in the evening. He missed Josée, Tessum, and Nansen, normal life, and the real world.

APRIL 21-22 (DAY SIXTY-FIVE). We've covered fifty-seven miles (105 km) in the past six days, a decent-enough rate, given the conditions we faced. But according to our schedule, we should have been making at least a mile (2 km) more per day. We didn't care; we knew that our speed would increase as our load lightened even more.

But the sun is now something of a disadvantage. Today Misha sensed the first signs of snow blindness and hurriedly put on his sunglasses. The pain ceased, but tears ran down his cheeks this evening. Still, we managed another 12.5 miles (23.1 km), an indication that the ice is changing in our favour.

APRIL 22-23 (DAY SIXTY-SIX). A twenty-nine-hour working day that left us tired, but not exhausted, even though Richard nodded off during the final rest break.

We received a message via TUBSAT that Rick Sellick and his colleagues are going to Ward Hunt to retrieve the HEALTHSAT unit. Then they plan to fly north and attempt to locate our position, so as to take photos with a new digital camera. Deb Hine advised us to smile when the plane was overhead. During the second march, we heard its engines in the distance. We caught a glimpse of it amid the clouds, but suddenly it turned aside, missing us by at least a mile, and flew back southward again. Presumably the pilots were working on coordinates from yesterday. It was strange to think that Rick, Karl Zeberg, and the others on board were so close, but might as well have been on the other side of the world. We wanted so badly to talk to them, but we had no way of contacting the plane directly, and the TUBSAT would have taken too long. Even a fly-over would have been great. Just to see another human responding to us.

APRIL 23-24 (DAY SIXTY-SEVEN). A beautiful day, with lots of sun, no wind, and a temperature of $-20°C$ ($-4°F$). The only thing that slowed us was a patch of fog that appeared quite suddenly and did not last for long. We covered 13.5 miles (24.9 km) and drifted another 0.5 mile (1 km) north during the night. We were closing in on 87°15', but there was no rest for the explorer. Misha, a fan of classic films, said that he felt like the Tin Man from *The Wizard of Oz*. He longed to be taken apart, thoroughly lubricated, and put together again.

APRIL 25-26 (DAY SIXTY-EIGHT). Over our morning coffee, we studied maps, in efforts to figure out what was beneath us on the ocean floor. We saw that we were nearing the Lomonosov

Ridge. Soon we'd be directly above its highest peaks, which would intensify the southern and easterly drift. Our aim was to get past this point as quickly as possible. North of 89° the drift would moderate, and we could afford to stop, gather our strength, and make the last push for the Pole. Looking at a map, it all seemed very easy.

Later we got a TUBSAT message asking us to test the Argos beacon. We hadn't switched it on since we left the storage depot; so there'd been no way for anyone to verify the positions we'd been reporting. Chances are that no one believes our progress. At first we were bogged down, making only about five miles (9 km) daily; but lately we'd been racing along at a tremendous clip, reaching 87°30' in the wink of an eye.

"Besides," said Misha, "the plane did not see us day before yesterday. For all anyone knows, we could be anywhere."

"That's true," said Richard. "Think about it. The last person who actually saw us was Og MacKenzie, when we were heading off. His sleds were as big as moving vans. He probably thought that we were the ones who were crazy, marching to the Pole with what looked like a quarter of his load. And who'd believe us if we told them that we actually left some of our things behind at 84°?"

No one, that's who – but we decided there was no great need to prove ourselves by turning on the Argos beacon (which, by the way, cost $45 (U.S.) each time it sent a signal to the world outside). We thought we'd make our friends rely on our own good word, and switch it on only when we neared the Pole. That's the best place to confirm our story.

APRIL 26-27 (DAY SIXTY-NINE). One of our metal fuel cans sprang a leak, and we poured its contents into a plastic fuel container brought for that purpose. The wind was negligible, but we continued to drift eastward about 0.1 miles (0.2 km) an hour.

APRIL 27-28 (DAY SEVENTY). Dense fog slowed our progress across a large, flat pan. We had no reference point, which drove Misha wild; he likes to see where he's going. Richard didn't mind; what made him feel uneasy was a white-out. We stopped every ten minutes and checked the compass, then pressed on. But fog makes the mind wander off on its own byways. While napping during a rest break, Richard dreamt that the expedition was over. He was back at Basil's hotel in Resolute, looking at an Arctic picture book with his children on his knees. Then Misha said, "It's time to go," and snapped him back to reality.

APRIL 29 (DAY SEVENTY-ONE). A rest day, with eleven hours of much-needed sleep, lounging in our sleeping bags with sukhari (dry Russian raisin bread) and butter. The ice around us was in constant motion. Richard went outside in the early morning to defecate. By mid-afternoon, the spot he'd chosen was separated from the tent by thirty metres (98 ft.) of water.

Tomorrow we shall begin our dash for the Pole. We hope to reach it in ten days, travelling thirteen miles (24 km) a day. This ought to be possible; we've averaged 12.5 miles (23.1 km) daily for almost a week. It may be coincidence, but Robert Peary began his final push from this same latitude – 87°47'. He claimed to have reached the Pole and returned to 87°47' in ten days. We can't do that, but then probably neither did he; no expedition had made such speed on the Arctic Ocean for one, let alone ten days. At least we can confirm our arrival at the Pole.

CHAPTER SEVENTEEN

MAY 1-2 (DAY SEVENTY-THREE). Today we covered 15.4 miles (28.5 km), aided by a favourable drift, and reached 88°15'. This took us eight marches, and we were on our feet for almost fifteen hours, stopping for only twenty minutes at a time.

Richard grew very tired by the end of the seventh march, and the final march was very unpleasant indeed. Counting the time it takes to break camp in the morning and set up again when we stop, our days have often exceeded twenty hours. Extreme fatigue sets in, and the last two marches are always much less productive than the preceding six. Today this led to an acrimonious exchange when Richard called a halt ten minutes early, at what seemed to be a good campsite. "Why are you stopping?" Misha asked. "Because I'm tired," Richard said. "You're supposed to be tired," said Misha. "We've chosen this eight-march regime, and we can't change."

Richard believed that Misha's attitude was unnecessarily uncompromising and doctrinaire, but Misha disagreed. His diary records his belief that the point at issue was "a matter of psychology. Richard is more emotional and sensitive. He could not reconcile himself to the monotony of our life. It was easier for me; I am more rational, steady, thick-skinned. We could not afford to give way to our emotions. We were in good physical condition; we still had the necessary stamina. We had to summon up our will every day, but we had not yet exceeded our limits. We just had to stand it." Richard was not convinced of this, and would return to the issue again.

MAY 2-3 (DAY SEVENTY-FOUR). We crossed one lead today on soft, spongy ice. We skied with legs spread wide to distribute our weight, gliding slowly and steadily, avoiding jerky motions. Our movement sent waves through the ice.

When it was his turn to set the pace, Richard deliberately slowed down and found that he was less exhausted at the end of the day. But both of us remained on edge, speaking less openly; the strain between us is evident and has to be dispelled.

MAY 3-4 (DAY SEVENTY-FIVE). We talked about the day before yesterday, when our tempers had flared over stopping ten minutes early. To Richard, ten minutes after fourteen hours was irrelevant. To Misha, it seemed to be a point of principle. He also felt tired, but denied his feelings. In effect, he said to his own body, "You are wrong. You will walk." Then he awaited a more serious sign of fatigue. In his mind, to do otherwise was the first sign of "giving in," which would lead to more frequent compromises. The next day, we would be tempted to stop twenty minutes early, and so forth and so on.

Richard had heard these arguments before, and saw things differently. Misha might be the physically stronger, but Richard was the more experienced skier. He had learned to trust his body; he knew when he was too tired. It was all very well to be persistent and prevail over the forces of nature, but there was no sense in going to the wall every minute of every day. Fighting off extreme fatigue for hours on end was counterproductive; our time could be spent to far greater effect if we simmered down a bit. Frankly, he was upset by Misha's very boring insistence that it was "all in his head."

In any case, today was a typical "survival day" — absolutely colourless, hard slogging in white-out conditions. We covered 10.8 miles (19.9 km), but overnight the accursed drift would send us 1.2 miles (2.2 km) back.

MAY 6-7 (DAY SEVENTY-SEVEN). This morning we crossed the Lomonosov Ridge, but kept drifting southward at 0.1 miles (0.2 km) an hour. We could see nothing in the grey, lustreless light. It's worth going to the Arctic if only to grasp what "hell on earth" is all about. We plodded on another 11.5 miles (21.3 km), and reached 89°, but the drift robbed us of almost an entire mile (2 km). At least the movement of the ice will abate as the ocean beneath us deepens. According to our charts, it was already 3,000 metres (2 mi.) to the bottom – twice as much as a few days ago.

We received a blaze of imperative messages from the outside world. Paul Lavelle's read: "Charge!" Robert Swan, our fellow explorer, had written: "Attack!" Pat Doyle, the First Air pilot, sent general greetings. We responded, saying that we'd be back at Ward Hunt by June 13, plus or minus a couple of days. How unpleasant, knowing that every fraction of a mile's drift delayed that arrival.

Resting after one of the marches, Misha fell asleep, and in his dream was visited by his mother, who asked him if he was all right. Her presence was so real, her voice so clear, that he was going to reassure her, when he suddenly awoke and realized where he was.

MAY 7-8 (DAY SEVENTY-EIGHT). We came across two sets of tracks: one belonged to Will Steger's expedition and the other was Paul Shurke, who'd also marched with Steger in 1986. Shurke was taking an easy and abbreviated route with a group of paying guests. "Wilderness, indeed!" snorted Misha. "The place is flooded with tourists!" Their trail was plain to see, because they were travelling by dogsled. This afternoon a strange message arrived from Josée. She apologized that she had not kept her "promise about the rabbits good for kids – see you soon." Rabbits? Richard could recall no promise concerning rabbits, but was cheered that she was in good spirits – more than could be said for us. In the afternoon, we came upon a very lengthy crack. We moved along it for two solid hours, but could not find a crossing place. Richard suggested that we use our inflatable boat, but Misha pointed out that the water was full of razor-sharp shards of ice. "Let's save it for emergencies," he said. Only by the end of the day did the crack narrow sufficiently for us to hopscotch across, jumping from one floating piece of ice to another. When we made our camp, only forty-eight miles (89 km) remained to the Pole.

MAY 8-9 (DAY SEVENTY-NINE). A day of celebration for Misha – the fiftieth anniversary of Russia's WWII victory over the Nazi invaders. In Moscow, the May Day parade would be winding its way through the streets, a display of military might. A message came via TUBSAT, reading: "Our thoughts are with you and Richard. We toast you and your forthcoming victory. Olga and Ryazan." How very nice – but May 9 was also the birthday of Tessum, Richard's son. "You are not here now, are you?" said Misha. "You are at home with your family." "Yes," Richard replied. "And Josée's birthday is May 20. I'm so sorry I can't be with them."

But what were ordinary, familiar days to us? During the night we drifted 0.7 miles (1.3 km) north but more than three miles (6 km) east. Only thirty-three miles (61 km) remained to the Pole; that was the important thing. Then, having reached it, the time would fly. Everything would go so quickly – the days, the food, the miles to Ward Hunt. So on we went, through yet another white-out that made us feel as if we were skiing in outer space.

MAY 9-10 (DAY EIGHTY). More unprecedentedly vile weather – totally unlike our previous experiences at this time of year. The three North Pole Light trips, Steger's expedition, and Polar Bridge had all enjoyed clear sailing at the end of April and in early

May. Whenever the wind picks up, the ice begins drifting more rapidly than ever. That is fine if it carries us north; dangerous if we are swept so far east that we enter the Greenland current. As before, we point not towards the Pole but 15° to the left to overcome this eastward drift.

So rapid is our progress that we can actually be at the Pole the following day! If we make good time, and the drift continues, we might cover fifteen miles (28 km) before making camp. That would leave a mere five miles (9 km) to go! Our plan is to leave our gear behind, march with only our backpacks to the Pole, and return as quickly as we can. Today we saw a bird – a good omen at last. It looked like a large black and white sparrow. It hovered above us, tweeting merrily, and then disappeared back towards land. Another wonderful realization dawned – we, too, would soon be turning south.

MAY 11-12 (DAY EIGHTY-ONE). This is the day we'd worked for for so long; our journey seems to have started a thousand years ago. But the day itself was very long as well – a total of more than forty hours from start to finish.

We slept poorly, filled with anticipation, but felt refreshed when we arose. We made seven marches, checking our coordinates with extra care. Richard kept the GPS under his clothing, warmed up and ready to go.

We made camp at 89°54', surrounded by cracked ice. The sun broke through for the first time that day, as if it wanted to share our triumph. We ate half our dinner and napped for an hour, laying on our sleeping pads and using the bags as pillows. Then we set off with the GPS, the TUBSAT, the Argos beacon, and a videocamera.

Only six miles (11 km) remained to the Pole. We covered the distance quickly enough, even though a wind rose from the north, as if the Arctic couldn't resist placing one final barrier in our path. We left camp at 1 P.M. on May 12. Three hours later, we were standing on top of the world.

Now was the time to establish our presence beyond all doubt, for the benefit of the world outside. We left a symbolic ski track around an anonymous ice hummock and paced back and forth, trying to get the most exact reading possible. The GPS read: 89°59.93' – close enough for history. Richard held it up to the lens of the videocamera, then transmitted an Argos signal that was downloaded in Washington, D.C., and relayed to Ottawa, silencing the sceptics once and for all.

Were we emotional or festive? Not in the least. Indeed, the Pole was only a halfway point – the place where we turned around and headed back towards the real conclusion of the expedition, more than 400 miles (740 km) away. Only when we walked ashore at Ward Hunt would we have finally succeeded.

But for the moment, success was ours! We grinned and hugged one another, and Misha offered another Russia proverb, the motto "la vie moment." We "seized the moment" with a toast of our own. Instead of champagne, we'd brought with us a Thermos full of hot raspberry drink. So there we stood, unshaven and weary travellers, eating pemmican, bacon, nuts, and butter, and thinking about the long road home.

Fifty minutes after we'd reached the Pole, we took the first steps back down that road and found that Misha's proverb had been very apt indeed. Leaving all our gear and skiing the final six miles (11 km) to the Pole had been risky. Even as we returned to the camp, a storm was brewing; the wind had picked up and our tent was covered in snow. That night we would drift five miles (9 km) south, and the ice in the area would be smashed. If we had not sprinted to the Pole when we did, it would have taken us at least two more days.

We sent further messages via TUBSAT to our families, co-workers, sponsors, and friends – everyone who'd believed in and

encouraged us. We thought also of the Australian Dick Smith
and his offer of $200,000 to anyone who'd make an unsupported
return trip. Soon we could send word to him, inviting him to join
us at Ward Hunt. Our six-year-old dream was on the verge of
becoming a reality.

And one more point: When we first left camp, Richard
climbed a pressure ridge behind the tent and suddenly felt the
presence of our phantom friend. It had no gender; it wasn't a
man or woman. There'd been no sign of it since we left the
storage depot weeks ago. But here it was again, making a total of
three of us. The feeling was very powerful, very real; Richard felt
the hair stand up on the nape of his neck. For a long moment, he
didn't turn around, for fear that there'd actually be someone
standing there — a third person who wanted to come along for
the polar ride.

CHAPTER EIGHTEEN

MAY 12-13 (DAY EIGHTY-TWO). We awoke to a howling blizzard; the wind was driving us to the southwest at a good rate, but
the pressure ridges were building and fresh leads were opening up
in all directions. Today's marches went well, considering that the
previous day we'd been on our feet for thirty-one hours and
covered twenty-four miles (44 km) to the Pole and back to camp.
Indeed, we'd been wise to make a rush to the Pole. If we'd waited
a day, we might have been forced to camp again on the way up and
would almost certainly have run into badly broken ice in the
immediate vicinity of the Pole, wasted time trying to fix its exact
position, and lost a total of two, perhaps three days. This would
have meant that we'd have been unable to make it back to Ward

Hunt in time; so our decision to press on was absolutely critical to the expedition's success.

We made six marches of eighty minutes each and agreed that we would try to stick to this routine. We could not hope to extend our working day beyond fifteen hours very often; otherwise we'd cross over the verge of the possible.

Newly fallen snow impeded our progress, and we encountered leads the size of small lakes. Frequently, we could not see their other sides. We walked on undulating ice that threatened to give way beneath us, but we kept on going. At one point, we floundered amid a whirl of ice floes for two and a half hours — some of the most dangerous conditions we'd yet encountered. But we were inspired by the fact that our goal was almost in sight. For months we'd felt as if we were going God knows where; now we were going home.

MAY 14-15 (DAY EIGHTY-THREE). Only twenty-three days left, and we'll be on the shore of Ward Hunt. It's merely a matter of doing them one march at a time. Just get the job done, and try not to think about it too much. We're running on newfound adrenalin — the belief that we'll make it to the finish line. Even the weather improves — the sun breaks through, and we can discern colours and shapes, instead of white gloom and tedious, sinister blue. We were carrying far less weight, and felt like kids, free to play outside after a storm. Or, rather, free to work our passage, 365 miles (676 km) to the Ward Hunt ice shelf.

A message arrived from our expedition team, reading: "We hope you will succeed, and we are proud of you." They congratulated us on reaching the Pole — but even that seemed to have happened a thousand years before. We wanted so much to see them all in person — but we couldn't fly to the south like our friend the bird, as quickly as we did in our hopeful dreams. The key to our success was a sound strategy, and we debated the idea of making seven marches of ninety minutes each. An extra half-hour would take us 0.7 miles (1.3 km) down the line. By reducing the number of our working days, we'd increase the amount of food per meal en route. Substantial meals would help us move faster, even when the going was rough.

The temperature rose and reached 16°C (61°F) inside the tent. The black bag we hang from the roof, filled with snow that melts to provide us with water, now yields a whole litre (35 fl. oz.) overnight, unlike the usual two cups (18 fl. oz.). This saves fuel; we don't have to melt snow on our stoves. But the temperature outside climbs as well and will wreak havoc on the ice.

Today we covered 14.3 miles (26.5 km), but during the second march we had a narrow escape. While crossing a small lead, covered with young ice, we felt the surface start to go. Richard was leading the way, wary of telltale cracks in the snow cover that signalled the ice was bending and about to break. Suddenly, Richard went down. One of his feet entered the water, but he reacted instantly and managed to jump to a nearby frozen hummock. Misha wasn't so lucky. He'd been watching Richard and failed to see that he, too, was about to break through. Down he went, sprawled on the ice like a seal, and unable to extricate his left leg, which was soaked to the knee. In fact, we hadn't been skiing on solid ice at all. It was more like frozen slush, which is why we didn't notice the usual warning signs. It didn't bend; it just gave way without notice. Luckily, Misha's sled stayed put on a more or less solid surface behind him. He got his leg up onto the ice, crawled over to a more stable-looking floe, and sat there, cursing his fate and wringing out his socks and boot liners. The whole thing was yet another example of why one should be careful about voicing one's thoughts. Just the other day we'd been discussing spare clothing, and Richard had said that it was supremely unlikely that both of us would wind up in the water at the same time, each unable to help the other — the worst of all possible scenarios.

MAY 15-16 (DAY EIGHTY-FOUR). More haze, more leads and cracks both big and small that cut the surface into islands separated by thin ice and soft snow — the time-honoured Arctic obstacle course. We took turns leading to vary the monotony, but our mood was bleak. Misha had predicted this feeling of perpetual, numbing weariness and ennui. "We're going to feel like canned vegetables," he said. "They always taste the same to me — none is any saltier, spicier, or sweeter than another. We'll be the same way — neither more or less tired, just tired."

The only way out of this is to focus always on our goal. We have to be eager to accomplish it; everything hinges on our desire. To sleep longer or eat more will make us no stronger. A single day of rest will do no good — we need a week or nothing. To pause briefly will refresh us only for a matter of hours. Then the Arctic will grind us down again. We can't waste time; we have to keep on going.

MAY 17-18 (DAY EIGHTY-FIVE). Today we covered only 12.9 miles (23.9 km) after almost sixteen hours on our feet, marching into biting wind. We counted cracks as we went along — ninety-five of them blocked our way. One of them contained another seal, who poked his head out perhaps twenty-five metres (82 ft.) away. Richard prepared a rope and hook, while Misha grabbed the rifle. First he misfired; then aimed again but missed. The seal disappeared, then resurfaced farther away. It seemed to be taunting us, almost as if saying, "What a marksman!" But what a shame we didn't succeed in adding it to our food supply. Misha could almost smell the boiling ribs, and we agreed that the seal had missed a once-in-a-lifetime opportunity to become an official sponsor of the expedition.

MAY 18-19 (DAY EIGHTY-SIX). The wind drove us southward at 0.2 miles (0.4 km) an hour, bringing with it a dusting of snow.

The cracks began to freeze over, and our way became less difficult. We managed to cover an almost unbelievable 19.1 miles (35.3 km). A few more days like this and we'd be back on schedule. In the evening, we rechecked our supplies and found that we had twice as much powdered milk as necessary. We doubled our evening ration to sixty grams (2 oz.), which in itself made us feel absolutely full. We also found that we had more sweets than expected; now we can reward ourselves more frequently while making camp.

MAY 19-20 (DAY EIGHTY-SEVEN). Only eighteen working days left – although the number of calendar days remained to be seen. In any case, we had just enough food to last us that length of time, and therefore no desire to prolong the journey.

The white haze and dark clouds persisted, but we were being propelled southward by the wind with remarkable speed. Today we got a free ride of ten effortless miles (19 km), making a total of 105 miles (194 km) covered during the last six days. Many of the cracks had closed, pushed together by the wind, or filled with blown snow so that we could cross with ease. The ice has changed appearance as well. Now we were moving across thicker, older floes, which made for somewhat easier going.

But even now, as we neared our goal, we had to take care to preserve the unity of the team. It's hard to express our absolute reliance on one another for physical safety and mental well-being. It was a sort of polar marriage (for better or worse) – or, as Misha preferred, a brotherhood. To live in harmony with another person under such stringent conditions demands a certain etiquette – unfailing generosity and politeness. Tonight, for example, was hard on our nerves. The tent was buffeted by constant winds, and it was very difficult to sleep. Richard awoke, but drifted off again – unlike Misha, who was wide awake but lay motionless for a while, then silently prepared a meal while Richard logged nine much-needed hours of slumber. Another example: today our prepackaged breakfast was short one lump of sugar. Richard was counting on his customary two lumps – one with coffee, the second with porridge. But so was Misha, who habitually tossed both into his mug. This had happened before, and we'd split the third cube – but today Richard made the ultimate sacrifice, knowing that Misha had the sweeter tooth. A tiny gesture – just like our rule that whoever cooked would serve the other person. But small courtesies helped enormously to make the trip more bearable.

MAY 21-22 (DAY EIGHTY-EIGHT). All night long a strong wind had driven us 6.7 miles (12.4 km) south but 2.8 miles (5.2 km) to the east. Another free ride – but it also smashed the surrounding ice, and we were literally shaking in our beds. We awoke to a storm and decided to linger inside, drinking hot milk and soup. But the storm had blown us a visitor, and we heard an unfamiliar sound outside. At first we thought it was a dream, but then the tent roof trembled slightly and we heard a burst of song. Another bird! – which left its tracks in the snow around the tent and, with remarkable accuracy, its droppings splattered all over Misha's sled. It vanished before we could see whether it was the same bird that had circled us at the Pole, and we were forced to forgive its transgression. Lord knows that in the Arctic you take whatever chance you can to relieve yourself.

MAY 22-23 (DAY EIGHTY-NINE). An upbeat message arrived for Richard. Josée was delighted with her surprise birthday present, a soapstone carving that he'd bought in Iqaluit and sent back to Ottawa with the conspiratorial Michel Perron. She and the children had gone canoeing at the family cottage; they all awaited Richard's arrival home.

But both of us needed encouragement today. Misha felt as if his legs were empty, stripped of muscles and sinews. Weariness had sapped his strength, but we pressed on, with drastically lightened sleds that now contained only sixteen days' worth of supplies.

During one of the marches, we saw a dead bird beneath an ice hummock. Its body had melted the snow, creating a tiny indentation. It was cold, but not yet stiff; it had perished not long before. Was it the same bird that had visited us yesterday? Perhaps we should have fed it or opened the tent flap to see if it would fly inside and warm itself. Misha wanted to preserve its memory, and took a single feather from its tail. That feather will reach the shore its owner had failed to attain.

MAY 24 (DAY NINETY). A day from hell. We started out feeling tired, having slept badly, and everything went downhill. The sun emerged, and we skied in our underwear, sweating heavily. Our half-litre (18 fl. oz.) ration of water was insufficient; we felt dehydrated and disgruntled. Our skis would not slide in the soft snow, and we encountered large areas of broken ice. At the start of the final march, we were exactly 2.5 miles (4.6 km) short of our sixteen-mile (30-km) quota for the day. Misha was bound and determined not to stop until we'd covered this distance, but Richard failed to see the earth-shaking importance of tenths of miles. Again we began to argue. Misha insisted that we push ourselves, but Richard would have none of this and purposely lagged behind.

At least we reached a latitude of 87°11' – almost exactly halfway back to Ward Hunt and past the area of intense eastward drift. We planned, when we camped, to send a message to Dick Smith, inviting him to the island. But we could not do so; the TUBSAT's batteries had run down, and it failed to transmit. Richard hotwired two batteries together, but we contented ourselves with sending a message that explained our problems with the unit.

MAY 25-26 (DAY NINETY). We know that we are racing the spring breakup. If we average sixteen miles (30 km) a day, stopping only for short rests after we cross 83°, we should still be able to succeed — but who knows? If we were to return to the Pole today, we'd probably find it coming apart. Breakup starts in the north, and works its way south to where the ice is more solid and the drift is less. We must keep pace ahead of it, but we cannot ski much faster or longer at a stretch. Richard removed the inner layer of his polar suit. He has been too warm, which makes him sleepy and increases his sense of fatigue.

Today we finally succeeded in shooting a seal. In the morning, it had occurred to Richard that he wasn't eating enough. He was feeling constant hunger. He had lost weight; he was burning up his reserves of body fat, leaving nothing for the final dash. Then a seal appeared in one of the leads. Misha (the designated hunter) unpacked the rifle and fired but missed; he'd aimed a little too low. The seal dove to safety, but popped up again a minute or so later. This time, the bullet found its mark. But the wind blew the seal's body across to the opposite side of the lead, and we had to shovel in enough snow to make a bridge, cross over ourselves, and snag the carcass with a three-pronged hook. The seal wasn't particularly big, but it yielded about fifteen kilograms (33 lb.) of meat. We worked inside the tent, using our Swiss Army knives to cut open the skin, peel back the fat, and dice the meat into small cubes, leaving the skin on. We'd taken the tent floor out, so we dumped the entrails into a hole we'd dug in one of the corners. We kept the liver and boiled the bones and ribs with a package of instant onion soup mix. We ate the meat off several bones and packed the larger ones to take with us on the trail. It was all delicious.

We'd covered 9.3 miles (17.2 km) before we met the seal, and another 6.5 miles (12 km) in the afternoon. We were at a loss to choose a way through a hideous mixture of ice, snow, and water.

We'd spent eleven hours catching and butchering the seal, which made our working day almost twenty-nine hours long. But the extra food comes at an opportune moment. After eating cooked meat for supper, we feel less tired than before and really full for the first time in months.

CHAPTER NINETEEN

MAY 29-30 (DAY NINETY-FOUR). Severely broken ice plagued us all day long. Once, we had to climb an almost vertical wall that stood 2.5 metres (8 ft.) high. We lagged behind schedule, covering only 14.6 miles (27 km); Perhaps we will have to make an extra march each day.

MAY 31-JUNE 1 (DAY NINETY-FIVE). Soon it will be summer — a word that sounds remote and strange, given that we haven't yet encountered true spring. How many southern springs have we missed in exchange for adventures on the ocean of ice? But summer is coming to the Arctic, too, and the sun scorched us, the snow began to melt in a few spots, and icicles hung from the hummocks. Misha broke one off and tasted it. It was delicious, not salty in the least.

Unfortunately, the surface was no better than yesterday — riddled with cracks and open water. We made eight marches of two hours each, zigzagging to and fro, searching for a usable path. For every five minutes wasted crossing a crack, we could have skied about 0.2 miles (0.4 km). The young ice was covered with soft, crusty snow, and we kept bogging down. The remains of the seal meat varied our diet, but it didn't last long. Perhaps we would be forced to hunt again soon. Several times we noticed blow-holes in the ice, and, once, a trail of ripples appeared in a distant lead. Misha wanted to try his marksmanship again, but Richard was less enthusiastic. "I don't want to lug another dozen kilograms [25 lb.]," he said. "It's not the only seal in the Arctic Ocean; there'll be others on our way." Alas, we hadn't taken any of the first seal's fat, deceived by the fact that modern Inuit usually throw it away. Big mistake. We should have cut it into small lumps as well, to add to our soups. At least we were no longer dehydrated. By now the black-bag program was yielding eight litres (2 gal.) of water daily; we could take more with us at a time because we'd emptied out a coffee jar.

But soon we had other things to worry about. The entire day was an ordeal — 15.2 miles (28.1 km) over eighteen and a half hours. In the final half-hour, Misha again wanted to press on, looking for a better place to camp. Richard found this hugely irritating: in his view, one place was as good or bad as another, and an extra 200 metres (656 ft.) after almost twenty hours on our feet made absolutely no difference in the long run. Even Misha's explanation — "It's only natural; I want to be home sooner" — achieved nothing but further tension in the tent.

JUNE 1-2 (DAY NINETY-SIX). June, Arctic style: bright sun in a cloudless sky and a temperature of −6°C (21°F). We actually got sunburned and spent another day skiing in our underwear — two half-clad zanies, loose on the polar sea.

But by day's end, Richard had conceived another plan. "Let's leave the sleds behind," he said. "We only need the backpacks now."

Misha disagreed; he thought this premature. "Do you think we'll be able to make sixteen miles (30 km) a day with all that weight on our backs?" he asked. "I'm sick and tired of the sleds, too; we can go faster without them. But we're not as strong as before. Haste may be dangerous. Let's wait for a couple of days and see what happens."

Again we worked for more than eighteen hours at a stretch. Once, Misha was leading the way and weakened the ice on the far side of a crack as he stepped across. Richard followed, but the bank began to crumble beneath him, and he had to throw himself forward to avoid a ducking. The second incident was rather more serious. Richard was leading on thin, snow-covered ice. The whole surface started to give way, and his sled got stuck behind him. He couldn't pull, because the movement would force him down. Nor could he retreat, because his skis were already in the water. He braced himself with his ski poles as Misha came up behind him and hung onto the sled until he regained his feet.

Richard had had enough and announced that the next day he would abandon his sled and transfer all his load to his backpack. Misha pointed out that, if he did so, he would quite likely die, destroying both himself and the expedition. Richard felt that Misha was deliberately setting out to annoy him so that he would see the error of his ways. But Misha was never a fan of backpacks; nothing could change his basic preference. He said, "You are getting weak psychologically," which did not achieve the desired effect. Richard felt that there was nothing psychological about it. The onset of fatigue after eighteen hours of hard work wasn't weakness of any kind. As an athlete, he knew his body; he also knew that his and Misha's capabilities were different. "It's fine for you," he said. "You start off slowly and feel better and better throughout the day. You build up; I run down. When I'm this tired, my judgement starts to fail me. I don't want to burn out and get sloppy. I'm working inefficiently, and it's got to stop. I'm not going to make it to Ward Hunt if you insist on thirty-eight-hour days." Now it was Misha's turn to become indignant. "What can I do?" he cried. "You will collapse under your pack." Richard said that he didn't think so, but that he was going to find out, and after a hot though inconclusive discussion, we went to bed. These bickerings were a clear sign that we were coming to the end of our rope. We'd suffered so much – but now that there was light at the end of the tunnel, the physical and emotional strain was beginning to show. Trifles made us miserable, and the slightest bit of luck brought almost undue elation.

Later that night, Misha proposed yet another variant on the plan. This harked back to his experiences during Icewalk, when the expedition had once made a dozen marches of an hour each. Perhaps if we made a larger number of shorter marches, we'd grow less tired and require shorter rest periods. Richard agreed to give it a try, and Misha went so far as to suggest that he should take the lead more often at the end of the day, when he felt the stronger. We had to speak plainly, even at risk of hurt feelings, and help each other to attain the common goal.

That night Richard wrote in his diary: "Misha is really a very good partner. The end of the journey has been harder on me physically. I lack his endurance, his ability to plug away for eighteen hours at a go. We may disagree, but he's been extremely patient and considerate – and I do my best to be considerate to him. I guess that's what makes a partnership. For example, today we came to a narrow lead. We could step across, but the far side was higher, with a questionable-looking edge. Misha said, 'I don't feel comfortable; I can't do this.' And I said, 'All right – I can.' Perhaps I had a better feel for it. So I went across, and then he was able to copy me. On the other hand, perhaps he has a better feel for thin ice than I do. Both of us are different; that's what makes a team."

JUNE 3-4 (DAY NINETY-SEVEN). In the morning, Richard began to transfer his load from sled to backpack, and found to his dismay that Misha had been right. The pack weighed in at at least

forty kilograms (88 lb.). It took only a few practice steps for him
to realize that even an hour's march with this monster on his back
would be beyond his powers, so all the supplies went back into
the sled. End of discussion.

Today was clear and sunny, but we were really skiing at "night."
Although the sun never set, the snow conditions were noticeably
different at night. The snow was cooler and transformed into
small ice crystals; we could ski faster and with far less effort.
When the ice was flat, our speed increased, and, once, we made
2.2 miles (4.1 km) in an hour. But this slowed to 0.1 miles (0.2 km)
when we found ourselves amid a marsh of ice. We tried to
hopscotch from one small floe to another, but a three-metre-wide
(10-ft.-wide) crack momentarily defeated us. We tried but failed
to shovel in a bridge as we'd done before, as the snow wasn't dense
enough and melted away. Finally, we turned our skis upside down,
used them to span the crack, and crawled across on top of them.

JUNE 4-5 (DAY NINETY-EIGHT). A dense fog fell, and water
overflowed the edges of the cracks, as if it were a tide. We had to
resort to yellow-filtered sunglasses; we felt like sports cars with
their fog lights on. We made good time, because all the snow that
had fallen recently had filled in the areas of broken and rough ice
and we could ski over the top. The fog stayed with us all day, but
we managed to cover another 18.8 miles (34.8 km) in less than
fifteen hours.

JUNE 6-7 (DAY NINETY-NINE). The temperature rose to zero,
stressing the need for speed if we were to stay ahead of the spring
breakup. To Misha's surprise, Richard suggested that we increase
our daily target from sixteen to eighteen miles (30 to 33 km). If we
succeeded, we'd arrive at Ward Hunt a day early. The island grew
closer with each passing hour. Only 93 miles (172 km) remained
to the ice shelf when we camped at 84°42'. A message via TUBSAT

confirmed that a plane had been booked and would pick us up at noon on June 15 – a week and a day away. "When we get to Ward Hunt, we'll make pancakes," Misha said. "We'll have a bath and wash away the smell of the seal."

We heard a seagull shriek and looked up to see it circling in the sky – a sure sign that land was near. But it might also signal that open water barred our path to the shore.

JUNE 7-8 (DAY 100). The ice grew worse and worse; cut with cracks and chequer-boarded with open water. Once, we commandeered an ice raft to ford an extremely wide lead. Richard used the hook with which we'd snagged the seal to catch a block of floating ice and pull it towards us. Misha was dubious – it measured ten by fifteen metres (33 × 50 ft.) and must have weighed several tonnes – but it slid through the water as if on ball bearings. We stepped on, pushed off with our ski poles, then tossed the hook onto the other bank and pulled ourselves across. The entire procedure took about forty minutes. Later we'd have to repeat it as the ice deteriorated.

Today we covered 18.2 miles (33.7 km), but our joy evaporated when a south wind began to blow, pushing us back where we'd come from. It was too soon for us to count on *nouvelle cuisine* (and, even more, *nouvelle* cleanliness) when we reached Ward Hunt.

JUNE 8-9 (DAY 101). Both of us spent a very restless night, and Misha rose often to check our coordinates. We were drifting north as if under full sail. The wind brought a mixture of snow and rain, soaking Misha's side of the tent. The interior temperature was 2°C (36°F). Water dripped morosely from the ceiling; it was impossible to sleep. Outside, the sky was hidden by dark, leaden clouds. We'd drifted 3.6 miles (6.7 km) overnight, back towards the Pole, which meant that we were bound to run into at least that distance of fresh, open water before we reached the ice shelf. Cracks were widening into leads in every direction. We could be delayed not only for hours but days.

Misha had taken a sedative and managed to fall into a heavy slumber. He awoke in the evening of June 8 and remembered that at least one bright spot awaited.

During the 1994 North Pole Light trip, Michel Perron had celebrated his birthday on the ice. His son Bertrand had presented him with a box of eleven chocolates – one for each person on the trip. Bearing this in mind, Michel and his wife, Lise, had given Misha a tiny package of chocolates for Richard's thirty-sixth birthday, June 9. Misha checked his watch and saw that three hours remained, but said, "Let's pretend that it's the ninth already. If you agree that it's your birthday, then it's time. Many happy returns."

First we shared a portion of sukhari, loaded up with butter. Then came two pieces of chocolate each; we saved the rest for our supper. For the past four months, we'd been sustaining ourselves on the same foods day in, day out – and here was something different, a reminder that good things, good friends, were awaiting us at our journey's end. The next day, a message arrived from Josée: "With you June 9. Cake awaits. Love from Mama and Papa and happy birthday from all."

CHAPTER TWENTY

JUNE 9 (DAY 101 CONTINUED). The word "weather" is inadequate to describe what was happening all around us. Noah's Flood seemed to have visited the earth again. We forded a five-metrewide (16-ft.-wide) crack by inflating our boat, but the crossing took us almost a solid hour. Everything was soaking wet; icicles were melting in the fog. The wind shifted into the southwest, driving us back and to the east, towards the Greenland current.

Clearly, we could not accomplish our eighteen-mile (33-km) goal. Our skis wouldn't slide; our average speed dropped from 1.6 to 1.2 miles (2.9 to 2.2 km) an hour, and we succeeded in covering only 11.6 miles (21.5 km) during eight marches. We devised a new plan (actually, a final dash): eight marches, two hours to set up camp and eat, four hours' sleep, two hours to eat and break camp, eight marches. Essentially no camp time, and much less sleep.

JUNE 9-10 (DAY 102). This morning we faced a fierce wind. Although the temperature climbed to zero again, we felt cold and put on our hooded windbreakers. Misha's hands were frozen stiff – his mittens had become so sodden that water dripped from them when he grasped his ski poles. The wind blew us off course, sending the sleds skewing wildly out of control.

Later the temperature began to drop, but the wind picked up again, until we had a serious blizzard. The wind, from the side, was so strong it pushed our sleds so that they were beside us, not behind us. Many times we were pushed off our feet and thrown to the ground. The ice became more treacherous, broken and smashed to bits, none of it flat anymore. Worse yet, it had begun to snow heavily. Visibility was zero much of the day. But we had no choice but to ski. We saw two ducklike birds – perhaps Arctic terns – swimming happily in a lead – a very strange sight in the middle of a blizzard.

We managed to cover 11.3 miles (20.9 km) in fourteen hours, but conditions were abominable inside the tent. The tent wasn't waterproof – as with our boots, you can't have it both ways. Either a fabric breathes or it doesn't. We'd opted for the former property – the right decision, at least until now. The seam where the two-part roof liner joined together leaked horribly, soaking our sleeping bags and pads, socks, and boot liners. Even the black bag we used to melt snow contributed to the deluge when it fell down into a pot full of water.

JUNE 10-11 (DAY 103). Four more hours of sleep. Today we crossed onto the continental shelf, where the ocean's depth rises abruptly from 300 to 1,500 metres (984 to 4,921 ft.). It's a shear zone, and the ice was incredibly shattered. We stopped drifting northward, although we continued to be pushed east all day long. But even that stopped by evening. We managed to cover another fifteen miles (28 km) amid rain, haze, and fog, skiing on almost completely saturated snow.

In the evening, we received a truly ridiculous message via TUBSAT. Somebody had come up with the bright idea that when we reached Ward Hunt and heard the pickup plane approach, we should rush out and frolic on the ice for the benefit of the film crew on board. These people simply don't realize what's happening. We are down to our last three days of food and fuel. The Arctic is falling apart as we look at it – we may not be able to reach Ward Hunt at all. If not, there's no way that an ordinary plane could land on the sink-hole slush. The only way to rescue us from drowning would be by means of helicopters – a major and very costly operation – and who knows where the nearest helicopter is based? We're skiing for our lives on four hours' sleep, and we have no patience with requests for photo opportunities! We know that our friends are looking at a map and thinking, "Well, they're so close; it's almost over and done." If only they were in our wet and painful shoes.

Richard looked at Misha and noticed for the first time that he was thin and drawn. His face had changed – the price exacted by our four-month battle against constant stress and hunger. Richard knew that he himself looked every bit as haggard underneath his beard. But the battle is almost won. We are so close – back now at 83°49', the site of our original storage depot. Surely we can summon up the necessary strength to complete our mission.

JUNE 12 (DAY 104). Now, in the final push, diary-keeping is the furthest thing from our minds. But later, when we attempted to reconstruct those days from memory, we found that we could replay the last stages of our journey with increasing accuracy, constantly interrupting each other with fresh detail.

Misha: "At night the ice had pressed together, but in the daytime it started falling to pieces. Just as we'd manage to get around one crack, another would bar our way, followed by countless others."

Richard: "But we coped with them for quite some time – until we came upon a small but very persistent crack that forced us to retreat. Striking out to right or left was no use; we seemed to be on a sort of ice peninsula. There was no end to the crack, and I suggested that we inflate our boat."

Misha: "We'd done this before, but not in such ice-congested waters. The boat seemed fragile and unreliable. The ten-metre-wide [33-ft.-wide] crack was filled with wet snow and ice. But Richard was determined. He unpacked and inflated the boat, which we'd christened *Fram* – the name of Nansen's ship. Our *Fram* would only take us one at a time, so Richard went across the crack first, because he's a better paddler. I expected that the boat would burst, but all went well, and we started to pull it back and forth with a cord, taking our gear – and me – to safety on the other side."

Richard: "The crossing took forty minutes. But ahead was really good flat ice; the cracks were narrow and packed with snow. Misha skied so quickly that I could hardly keep pace with him."

JUNE 12-13 (DAY 105). We covered thirteen miles (24 km) in six marches. It took us only six hours, two more than we'd planned.

We'd just decided to make camp and rest when Misha saw that the ice that lay ahead was a strange blue colour.

Richard: "It was land. Not much to look at, just a tiny speck on the horizon, but we could see land at last. We started to laugh and whoop hysterically. I think I cried a little. We were so full of emotion. It was land – the end of the long road, and we knew that we could reach it.

"The clouds were low; they hid the mountain peaks. But there could be no mistake. The mountain that rises above Ward Hunt has a very distinctive shape; there's a V-shaped gully called a couloir that's filled with snow year-round. The white stripe could be seen from where we stood. It was the most wonderful sight I've ever seen in all my life."

Misha: "Now that we could actually see the distant shore, we didn't have to look at our compass to verify our route. Just as its pointer is attracted by a magnet, we were drawn to the island. It aroused in us a burning desire not to stop, to keep on going till the end."

Richard: "But reason prevailed; we had to stop and rest, to keep to our schedule instead of expending our strength in a mad headlong dash. We were only at 83°36' – the ice shelf remained twenty-eight miles [52 km] away."

We managed to sleep for only an hour and woke up excited but unrefreshed. Several marches brought us nearer to our destination. Our skis were sliding well enough at first, but things change rapidly, good luck never holds, and soon we found ourselves amid another tangle of broken, ragged ice.

Misha: "We were bogged down; the snow stuck to our skis. I knew we could not stand this for very long. Our legs were heavy – they could carry us, but not our gear and the awful weight of the clinging snow."

Richard: "The clock was running; the plane was due to pick us up in twenty hours' time. Misha kept saying, 'Look, we are making progress; the mountain is growing bigger.' But this seemed like self-delusion. I was about to suggest that we stop and rest, but Misha beat me to it."

Misha: "This was self-preservation, not self-delusion, at work. We were not behaving efficiently; there was no sense in tiring ourselves out. If we waited until evening, the snow would freeze and we could make better time. We'd covered only twelve miles [22 km], as opposed to the previous day's thirteen miles [24 km], so we were wise to rest and await a change in temperature."

JUNE 13-14 (DAY 106). During the night, we slept for only three hours, not wanting to waste more time. About 9 P.M. on June 13, we started off again.

Richard: "The expedition was almost over. The day to come would be the hardest and the longest of our journey. Strange, but fitting, that the Arctic would fight us tooth and nail even for those last few miles."

Misha: "We had a bad start; the temperature did not drop as we had hoped. Rather, it stayed just above the freezing point. Our premonitions were justified; reality turned out to be worse than we'd expected. Our skis were completely iced up; lumps of snow stuck to their bases. We were walking, not skiing. We made only 1.6 miles [3 km] during the first march. Sixteen miles [30 km] remained. We had to stand it, but how could we do so? Then I had a sudden revelation. When I was a boy, I used to wax my skis with a candle. For some reason, we'd saved a single candle from our supplies."

Richard: "We brushed off the snow, dried the skis as much as possible, and rubbed them with candle wax. What a difference this made! Perhaps we should patent the idea as a survival kit. The haze cleared, and we saw that the island was indeed closer. But the Arctic had one last surprise in store.

"At 3 A.M., beneath the midnight sun, we ran into a maze of

frozen ice rivers. I said, 'We're skiing beside a sleeping giant. The slightest noise will awaken him and the cracks will begin to open.' Five hours later, the giant stirred and the ice started moving with a hollow sound. We had to move forward; not even a helicopter could reach us where we stood. Any semblance of a solid, continuous surface had disappeared. Our skis were useless to us now; we put them into our packs and jumped from one insubstantial hummock to another. If we put a foot wrong, we'd feel the barely frozen slush give way."

Misha: "Finally, we reached a slightly larger floe. We had to rest and regain our concentration. I fell asleep at once and was lost to the world for two hours. Richard managed an uneasy rest of no more than an hour."

JUNE 14-15 (DAY 107). We started off again. The ice was completely smashed, all the pans reduced to tiny floes, with rivers of mush in between them. There was no end in sight. The first march, two hours long, yielded less than half a mile [1 km] of progress. Simple arithmetic showed we would miss our plane at this rate — but we could actually smell the land ahead of us. Without a word of discussion, we stopped and began to throw away our gear.

Richard: "First we got rid of the sled. Next came the tent's inner liner and floor, one stove, spare skis and poles, the video-camera and unused videotapes, the Thermos bottle, one pot and bowls, most of the first-aid and repair kits, clothing and personal belongings of every kind. For forty minutes, we littered the surface of the ice; our gear has joined centuries of jetsam at the bottom of the ocean. Now we could set off laden with only our backpacks and more than double our speed.

"Until we hit an ice wall standing three metres [10 ft.] high. On our way north, we'd called it the Great Wall of China. As we climbed it, we congratulated ourselves on leaving the sleds behind.

"Just beyond the wall, we once again encountered more loosely packed ice floes surrounded by rivers of tightly packed mush. We could walk on these rivers, but they would only support our weight for a second before we began to sink. Misha led the way; he has no rival when it comes to selecting the most likely stepping-stone."

Misha: "It's true – Richard is better at crossing cracks and leads, but I'm an expert on the ice itself. We leapt from one floe to another as if they were hummocks in a marsh or bog. We adopted a curious posture, moving like speed skaters, sliding quickly with half-bent knees. The ice shelf was very close; we could see an old hut where the glaciologists used to live.

"The ice seemed to be more solid now, and we'd replaced our skis. I wanted to test the surface and bent forward to prod it with my ski pole. But I slipped and landed in a mixture of snow, ice, and water up to my waist. I was right to compare it to a marsh – it was sucking me down. I managed to get a grip on the edge, and cried, 'Richard, I can't get out of it! I may lose my skis.'"

Richard: "I stood for a moment, watching Misha sink down into the water. But I came to quickly. It seemed that he'd be able to get out if he unfastened his skis. But then they would sink, and we had no spares; we'd thrown them away. The surface was too thin for me to get close to him, so I took the spade, threw some pieces of ice into the water, put my skis on top of the slush, and used them to support me as I lay down. I rolled up my sleeves, stretched out my arm, and reached down under the ice to grab his skis."

Misha: "In any other circumstance, the sight would have been hilarious – one skier in the water; the other almost diving into it in a valiant rescue attempt. I was afraid that both of us would drown. Richard managed to get a hand on my skis and pull them to the surface. Now I could manoeuvre, and I crawled out, soaking wet. The wind was up, but we had no time to dry out.

Richard said, 'Are you cold?' 'What do you expect?' I said. 'But it doesn't matter — let's go.'"

Richard: "All around us the conditions were little better than the porridgelike slush we'd seen from the plane in 1992. Our skis kept breaking through the surface crust. We could see the shore very clearly now; it seemed that we would reach the ice shelf soon, if only we could cross a final pressure ridge."

Misha: "I climbed atop a large hummock and saw flat ice ahead. Richard skied up beside me. 'Why have you stopped?' he asked. 'Look over there,' I said. 'It's the ice shelf.' The time was two minutes past seven o'clock. 'Let's go side by side,' I said, and we slid down the ridge together."

Richard: "We couldn't help crying. We wept, leaning on each other's shoulder. We kept trying to say, 'We did it' — but we couldn't talk because of the lumps in our throats."

Misha: "Of course, it was merely a release from our weeks and months of endless stress. Now we could relax — even collapse — for the first time. We sat down on the ice shelf and searched our food packs. There was nothing left; no margin of error at all, only a few scraps of pemmican and bacon.

"We were exactly 200 metres [656 ft.] away from our starting point. When our team began to ask us, back at the end of April, when we would finish, we said that it could be anywhere from the 11th through the 15th of June. In the second half of May, they asked us again for an estimated arrival time, and we'd replied, the 13th of June — plus or minus a day. So here we were, on June 14th, seven hours and two minutes late."

Richard: "And with three miles [6 km] to go before we reached the hut. The ice shelf was dome-shaped; we had to climb over another rise. I was literally crawling, but Misha took off as if he had wings. I lagged far behind, thinking, 'Where does he get that energy? We've had only twenty hours' sleep in the past eight days.'"

Misha: "When Richard caught up, he asked, 'What's all the rush?' 'I'm just testing my legs,' I said, 'to see if they still work.'"

Richard: "When we came to the hut, we were surprised to see that someone had turned on the heat. Later we learned that the staffers from Ellesmere National Park had flown in the previous day on a wildlife survey. They left the heat on to make us welcome."

Misha: "Richard was walking zigzag, as if he were drunk. But I was doing the same. With the goal accomplished and our bodies starting to relax, our legs refused to behave in a normal fashion.

"For all those months, we'd dreamed of pancakes and coffee, of eating at a table like civilized men. But we were too exhausted. In two hours, all we did was make a cup of tea. Then we pulled off our wet clothes, got into heavenly dry sleeping bags, and slept for an hour and a half."

Richard: "You should have seen us trying to get up again! We crawled out of our bags like invalids, panting and groaning as we tried to assume a vertical position. We'd scarcely begun to pack our things when we heard the sound of an approaching plane."

Misha: "We ran from the hut and looked skyward. But no use! — the clouds hung too low for us to see. Suddenly, it appeared, and I started jumping and waving my hands like a madman. But then it vanished again behind the mountain peak.

"Later we learned that the plane had flown out, not knowing whether we'd arrived. As far as anyone knew for sure, our most recent coordinates were 83°11'. But my shouting and waving had been visible. The plane circled and came in to land. We ran to the landing strip, the door opened, and two small figures dashed to meet us — our wives, Olga and Josée."

Richard: "But plenty of others had come along for the ride. Soon we were hugging and shaking hands with Michel and Lise Perron, Jeff Mantell, Tim Kenny, Dave Adams (a student from the Follow Us project), Vladimir Mazaev, Candace Wilson, and Pat Doyle and his co-pilot."

With remarkable foresight, Josée had brought bottles of champagne, along with strawberries, cheese, cold cuts, and cake. It all smelled so wonderful – but we could taste so little. Our burned mouths and tongues had lost their sense of taste! We couldn't tell cake from ham, champagne from the raspberry drink that we'd consumed to celebrate our arrival at the Pole.

After we'd toasted our ultimate success, Michel showed us an imposing bronze sign that would be mounted where we stood. He'd had it manufactured while we were en route, confident that we'd merit the wording – which was, when it came to our arrival date, a trifle optimistic. But who was counting, when victory was ours? This is how it read, what you would read if you went tomorrow to the shore of Ward Hunt Island:

"This sign, raised by Michel Perron of Montreal, is dedicated to all explorers who have journeyed north to the Pole. Those who have travelled this ocean know the beauty and the harshness, the monotony and the unpredictability.

"June 7, 1995, marks the completion of the Weber–Malakhov expedition. On February 11, 1995, Richard Weber of Chelsea, Quebec, and Mikhail Malakhov of Ryazan, Russia, left this place carrying supplies for 110 days. They skied to the North Pole and returned, using only human resources and no outside assistance. This is the first successful unsupported surface journey from land to the North Pole and back to land.

"The Arctic Ocean always challenges those who attempt to cross its surface. It is a place where human physical and psychological limits are met and sometimes surpassed. Michel, Richard and Mikhail encourage people everywhere to push toward their own personal limits."

Michel concluded, "I hope this memorial sign will stand here for a thousand years."

Well, who knows what a thousand years will bring? We didn't care; we were going home – from Ward Hunt to Eureka, then to Resolute, Iqaluit, and Ottawa. Our fifteen minutes of fame began to pick up steam during the final flight. The pilot learned that we were on board and broke out champagne for everyone.

As soon as we stepped onto the tarmac in Ottawa, we were met by a media scrum, blinded by flashbulbs as if it were the Academy Awards. Our reputation had preceded us; even when we walked down the street, people would congratulate us and shake our hands.

We did it – that's all that need be said. Both of us were utterly spent, unable to travel anywhere for a period of time. We were so very tired – taxed to the limit if we climbed a flight of stairs.

But it was worth it. We'd shared an unbelievable journey, an amazing experience that neither of us will ever forget, one which we're unlikely to equal in our lifetimes. Each did it with the right person. We were a remarkable team, a sum greater than its parts. Misha says that we were – and are – polar brothers, and it's true.

We have no great desire to do it again – the ultimate case of been there, done that. We have other plans, other responsibilities. What we don't have is one single penny's prize money from Dick Smith, the Australian publishing magnate. We contacted him, and he was politely evasive. His response recalls a line from a John le Carré novel: "It never happened, and it was two other blokes." Which is fine – at least he got us going in the first place.

Time has passed, but the Arctic will not let us go. When we close our eyes for a moment, we find ourselves amid the ocean of ice. We struggle on, metre by metre; we can see the ice shelf and the island beyond. They seem so close, but in between are leads and cracks, and again we have to go around, climbing the pressure ridges and building fragile bridges from the snow, while the final shore remains unattainable.

EPILOGUE

After the first flurry of Arctic expeditions around the turn of the century, and after the great excitement they caused had died down, the North Pole was all but forgotten. It wasn't until aircraft capable of landing on the ice far out on the Arctic Ocean were developed that a new chapter in polar exploration began. Now that the odds of success were a little better, modern explorers became keen to follow in the footsteps of Fridtjof Nansen, Roald Amundsen, and Robert Peary. But, assisted by the new aircraft, they "forgot" about the return journey that was always an unavoidable part of their predecessors' expeditions. Just reaching the Pole was considered a feat; a return journey was impossible, even beyond comprehension. That was how we felt when we took part in our first expedition to the Pole, in 1986. It took all our power just to reach it – coming back was unimaginable. But in 1995, trading on our own ten-year apprenticeship in the Arctic, and on the thirty years of accumulated wisdom of modern explorers and scientists, we finally closed the historic circle and completed the original objective set by the earliest explorers.

It was a miraculous combination of good luck and good planning. When I look back, I am terrified at all the things that could have gone wrong. I cannot shake the fright of finding, one evening, that the alcohol in our thermometer, which went to -50, had dropped right off the scale; just a tiny red drop remained in the bulb at the bottom. There were days when I was so tired I could hardly put one foot in front of the other, and even after nine hours' sleep, we were still exhausted. I think in horror of how we shovelled snow into bridges over open water, skiing over them just fast enough to keep from sinking into the freezing black water.

And I remember the extraordinary flukes. When our skis were almost completely bogged down in soggy snow and badly in need of some wax, we were saved by the one extra candle we for some reason still carried, despite our practice of throwing all unnecessary equipment away. We reached land at seven in the morning, knowing that one hour later the ice in the final kilometre from shore would have started to move, and with a shift of just one centimetre or just a slight release of pressure, we would have been stranded on a tiny ice pan in a sea of slush. (Will Steger and his team were only thirty miles from land when we finished, but he had to have his dog team evacuated and his canoe-sleds brought in by aircraft. It took him two and a half weeks to complete that final thirty miles. A Korean team was only a few days behind us. They never made it to land and had to be evacuated by aircraft.) We never rationed our food, yet after four months, when we reached the ice shelf at Ward Hunt Island, only a few grams remained. They were promptly eaten.

Naturally, anyone setting out on an expedition of this magnitude carries with them a vision of their possible triumph. And even if they are successful, reality is often twisted by circumstances beyond their control and bears little resemblance to what was imagined. For a year and a half, Wally Herbert lead one of the greatest modern expeditions across the Arctic Ocean, but his success, in July 1969, was totally eclipsed by Neil Armstrong stepping onto the moon. Our expedition was no exception. After our success, the National Geographic Society could not, it seemed, overcome their bias and accept that we have serious doubts that Peary, an American, ever made it to the Pole. Their magazine featured instead an American expedition that had made the first five hundred kilometres of its polar journey by helicopter, and had been resupplied by aircraft twice. Even their leader called it a "non-expedition." When *National Geographic* did cover our expedition, they gave it three sentences in the January 1996 issue, where the supposedly scientific body claimed that our success was due to eating chocolate-covered truffles. Even then, they compared our expedition with Peary's, although in almost every aspect the two are completely unalike.

We have been more fortunate in our own countries. In Russia, President Yeltsin presented Misha with the title "Hero of Russia." He is the first Russian civilian to be so honoured. And I will receive the Order of Friendship of Nations, the highest award permissible for a foreigner. The Canadian government has awarded both of us the Meritorious Service Medal for out-standing achievement.

The recognition is nice, but now we have both moved on with our lives. Misha has embarked on a career in politics. He finished a close second in a bid to win a seat in the Russian parliament during the 1995 federal elections. His campaign slogan was "I am proud to be from Ryazan." In January 1996, he helped organize candidates for local elections in his area, and in the summer he worked for Yeltsin's re-election. Russia's new democracy needs people with Misha's vision and experience.

My dream is to work with my wife, Josée, to build a wilderness lodge on Baffin Island in the Canadian Arctic. It will be a comfortable place from where guests can ski, ocean kayak, hike, watch wildlife, go dog-sledding, or just relax. And I will continue to lead adventure trips in the Arctic.

Whatever we do and wherever we go, Misha and I will always be Polar Brothers. Together, we shared a vision, of our journey and of our finish at Ward Hunt Island. We conceived a plan that accounted for every tiny detail, from the calories in our herbal tea to the drift of the Arctic ice in February, ninety miles from land. And, hardest of all, we persevered. Holding onto our vision and our plan, and believing in them always, we persevered.

Misha and I think that our feat will not be matched for the next few years, but we throw out the challenge to anyone who wishes to repeat it. We salute you and wish you the best of luck.

Richard Weber

APPENDIX A

1995 EXPEDITION EQUIPMENT LIST

Item	Brand/Model		
skis	Fischer E99 Crown	2.5	pairs
poles	Swix Alulight	3.5	pairs
bindings	Canadian Military	5	pairs
bindings	Berwin	4	pairs
backpack	Ostrom Outdoors	4	
vest, fleece	custom/Malden Mills Polartec	2	
jacket, fleece	custom/Malden Mills Polartec	2	
polar suit, pants	custom/Malden Mills Polartec	2	
polar suit, jacket	custom/Malden Mills Polartec	2	
wind pants	custom	2	
wind jacket	custom	2	
underwear, fishnet	Tarramar	8	sets
underwear, med. weight	Tarramar	4	sets
underwear, expd. weight	Tarramar	4	sets
boots	Kaufman, Sorel Expedition	2	pairs
tent boots	custom	2	pairs
socks	Thorlo Winter Liner	12	pairs
socks	Thorlo Extreme Winter	6	pairs
expedition mitts	Paris Gloves	3	pairs
expedition gloves	Paris Gloves	2	pairs
Syntan gloves	Paris Gloves	2	pairs
headcover	custom	2	
hat, fleece	custom	2	
hat, fur	Winnipeg Furs	2	
earmuffs	Swix	1	
sunglasses	Bollé, Edge II	2	
sunglass lens	Bollé, red & yellow	4	
pocket knife	Swiss Army Knife	2	

sleds	custom	8
sled bags	custom	8
towing system (carabiners and rope)	custom	4
bowls (stainless steel)		2
cups (plastic)	Owl Rafting	2
spoons, eating	Lexan	2
spoon, cooking	Lexan	1
stoves	MSR (1), Coleman (2)	3
pot, 6 litre, for water (aluminum)		1
pot, 4 litre, for cooking (Teflon)		1
heat exchanger	MSR	2
Thermos (stainless steel)	Thermos	1
wood board	custom	1
pot jacket	Traveling Light	1
sleeping bag	RAB Down Equipment	2
VBL bags	custom	2
sleeping pads	Cascade Designs, Ridge-Rest	2
camp chairs	Crazy Creek	2
tent	custom	1
snow shovel	Mountain Shovel	1
snow saw		1
boat, inflatable	(Russian made)	1
seal hook	Iqaluit	1
first-aid kit	custom	1
rifle, 308	Cullity Restorations	1
ammunition	Sportsmart	20 rounds
TUBSAT	U of Berlin	2
Argos beacon	NACLS	1
navigation, GPS	Garmin Navigation	2
repair kit	custom	1

video camera (Hi-8)	Sony	2
camera	Nikon FM-2	1
camera	Leica	1
drill	custom	1
trail flags		
(bamboo and black nylon)		200
locater beacon	Televilt	1
trip wire and bear scares	British made	3

APPENDIX B

1995 EXPEDITION DAILY DIET
(a slightly refined version of the 1992 daily diet)

BREAKFAST	Calories per 100 gm	Grams	Total Calories
oats, instant	346	90	311.40
sugar	385	24	92.40
nuts (macadamia)	775	50	387.50
milk (dry)	600	60	360.00
Shaklee Vitalea (multivitamin and B-complex)	0	3	0.00
coffee (instant)	100	6	6.00
total grams and calories		233	1 157.30

LUNCH			
butter	716	124	887.84
bacon (double-smoked)	650	100	650.00
nuts (Brazil 25%; pecan 40%; walnut 15%; filbert 15%; cashew 5%)	712	100	712.00
chocolate truffle with macadamia nuts	650	100	650.00
dry bread, Russian	420	20	84.00
sport drink, Shaklee	366	25	91.50
candy	364	5	18.20
total grams and calories		474	3 093.54

SUPPER	Calories per 100 gm	Grams	Total Calories
pemmican, beef (644 Cal/100 g) or chicken (623 Cal/100 g)	633	200	1 266.00
cheese, cheddar (dry)	614	35	214.90
cheese, St. Andre	775	15	116.25
crème fraiche (dry)	775	75	581.25
pasta (383 Cal/100 g) or rice (363 Cal/100 g)	373	133	496.09
milk (dry)	600	50	300.00
tea	1	3	0.03
total grams and calories		511	2 974.52

DAY'S TOTAL GRAMS AND CALORIES		1 218	7 225.36

Note:

1. Average calories per 100 g of food: 576

2. We found that breakfast was not substantial enough, so throughout most of the expedition we reserved about a third of our supper to eat with breakfast.

APPENDIX C

1995 DAILY LOG

Our 1995 Daily Log has 111 entries in 26 columns. It required three pages laid side by side to include all 26 columns. We had fewer columns of information in 1992. The entries for each day are as follows:

Date: Calendar date during the expedition.

Day: The number of days into the expedition. An expedition day can be longer than a calendar day, because during most of the expedition there was 24-hour sunlight. In such conditions one can arbitrarily chose the length of each day.

A.M. Lat: Latitude in the morning upon waking up.

A.M. Long: Longitude in the morning upon waking up.

P.M. Lat: Latitude in the evening after setting up camp.

P.M. Long: Longitude in the evening after setting up camp.

Progress: Progress made during the day in our desired direction. It is the evening position minus the morning position.

Drift (lat/long): This is the distance we drifted during the night. It is the difference between the position recorded the previous evening and the morning position. It is recorded in the north-south direction in nautical miles (minutes) of latitude and in the east-west direction in degrees and minutes of longitude. It should be noted that one minute of longitude becomes a shorter and shorter distance as one approaches the Pole. For example, at 84° north, one minute of longitude is 0.105 nautical miles; but at 89° north, one minute of longitude is only 0.017 nautical miles. (There are 60 minutes in a degree of latitude and longitude.)

A.M. Drift+2hrs (lat/long): This is the distance we drifted in two hours from the time we woke up in the morning. It is expressed in the same manner as the overnight drift.

P.M. Drift+1hr (lat/long): This is the distance we drifted in one hour after we recorded the evening position. It is expressed in the same manner as the overnight drift.

No. of Marches: The number of marches we did during the day. At one point Richard started recording the number of rests.

Lngth Marches: The length of each march measured in minutes. Time spent reconnoitring or spent crossing cracks or pressure ridges was not included.

Start Time: The time we started skiing each day. We stayed on Eastern Standard Daylight Savings Time for the duration of both expeditions.

Finish Time: The time when we stopped skiing and made camp each day.

Working Time: The length of our working day, expressed in hours and minutes. Calculated by subtracting Start Time from Finish Time.

Rise Time: The time we awoke in the morning.

Bed Time: The time we went to sleep each night.

Hrs Sleep: The length of time we slept, expressed in hours and minutes.

Day Hrs: The number of hours in our "day." This was calculated by subtracting the Rise Time from the next Rise Time. In 1992 it was calculated by subtracting the Start Time from the next Start Time.

A.M. Temp: Temperature in the morning, expressed in degrees Celsius.

P.M. Temp: Temperature in the evening.

A.M. Wind/Direction: Wind speed and direction in the morning. The speed was estimated. In 1992 it was in kilometres per hour, and in 1995 in metres per second. We think that we were consistent throughout each expedition. However, the speeds seem low for 1992. It was very hard to estimate the wind speed when the wind was very strong.

P.M. Wind/Direction: Wind speed and direction in the evening.

A.M. Weather: Description of the weather in the morning.

P.M. Weather: Description of the weather in the evening.

Ice Conditions: A description of the ice conditions that we encountered that day.

Here is an example of the entries for one day:

DATE	A.M. LAT	A.M. LONG	P.M. LAT	P.M. LONG	PROGRESS (MILES)	DRIFT (LAT/LONG)	A.M. DRIFT +2HRS (LAT/LONG)	P.M. DRIFT +1HR (LAT/LONG)
May 5	37°0'	79°08'	49'5°	77°58'	12.6	1.0S\35W	.1S\6'W	.1S\1'E

NO. OF MARCHES	LNGTH MARCHES	START TIME	FINISH TIME	WORKING TIME	RISE TIME	BED TIME	HRS SLEEP	DAY HRS	A.M. TEMP
8	75–80	04:05	17:25	13:20	00:15	22:30	8:25	28:40	-8

P.M. TEMP	A.M. WIND/ DIRECTION	P.M. WIND/ DIRECTION	A.M. WEATHER	P.M. WEATHER	ICE CONDITIONS
-14	3-4 ESE	2-3 ENE	overcast, whiteout	visible sun, semi-whiteout	old pans with short loose rough area, some young ice, detour 1 crack for 2 marches

The full 1995 expedition log is available to interested parties. Please send a stamped, self-addressed 9×12 envelope to Polar Attack 1995 Log, McClelland & Stewart Inc., 481 University Avenue, Toronto, Ontario, M5G 2E9.

APPENDIX D

ROBERT PEARY

Time and again on our three polar expeditions, we talked about Robert Peary and his journeys in 1906 and 1909. By June 1995, having crossed between Canada and the North Pole five times, we had gained far more experience travelling on the Arctic Ocean than anyone in history, and about four times more experience than Peary. We feel that we are uniquely qualified to draw certain conclusions about Peary's expeditions. While these conclusions are not necessarily new, they have never been corroborated with so much practical evidence.

It is not possible to reach the North Pole without checking longitude and making adjustments for drift, and in all our expeditions we have always had to make considerable corrections to compensate for the movement of the drifting ice. The ice, especially in the area of the North Pole, moves an average of three miles (6 km) per day; if it is windy, as Peary describes in his book, drift will be as much as ten to fifteen miles (19 to 28 km) per day. It is never due south or north, except for short periods as the wind shifts. Drift, especially if accompanied by wind, can consequently destroy a trail in one night. Near our Pole camp we found that our trail had moved relative to our camp as much as one kilometre and had rotated almost ninety degrees.

Most data on ice shift is very general, gathered by drifting ice stations and remote sensing buoys. Only since the arrival of the GPS, in 1990, have expeditions been able to describe with any accuracy the extent to which drift affects a party travelling on the ice.

There are some who would argue that Peary had vast experience; he had, after all, spent years in the Arctic – much of his adult life. He was indeed a very experienced explorer, but *not* in travel on the Arctic Ocean. Before the start of his 1909 expedition, Peary had spent only about forty days on the Arctic Ocean, about the same amount of time as had Bob Mantell. Conditions in Greenland or elsewhere in the Arctic cannot prepare one for travel across the Arctic Ocean. Note that when Reinhold Messner – without doubt the greatest mountain climber of the twentieth century, but with no experience of the Arctic Ocean – attempted to travel to the North Pole, he and his expedition made only eleven miles (20 km) before his expedition was thrown into havoc by shifting ice.

Not only was Peary a novice, he was without the benefit of the accumulated scientific knowledge of the last ninety years. He was a true explorer, going where no one had been before, and so had no knowledge of what might await him at the Pole. Knowledge of drift at the time was very sketchy; nothing at all was known of the bathometry of the ocean; and Peary didn't know about the continental shelf or the Lomonosov Ridge and their effects on the ice.

Some people claim that Peary's companion, Matthew Henson, could estimate within a mile the distance he had travelled each day. This is impossible with the stop-and-go nature of Arctic Ocean travel. What is more, novices (and Henson, too, falls into this category) tend to overestimate the distance they have travelled. They get caught up in the rigours of the journey and lose track, or they inflate the distance travelled in their minds, just to cheer themselves up. We now have the GPS. Every evening we can turn it on and tell exactly how far we have gone that day. After the last two expeditions, we can estimate with about 20 per cent accuracy our daily mileage. But this is only because we have been able to practise with a GPS each day for eight months, and sometimes we have still been unpleasantly surprised. During the Steger and Polar Bridge expeditions, both before 1990, we were unable to guess how far we had travelled each day. Not even the Inuit can tell you how far you're going on the ocean. They measure the distance in "sleeps." It's almost Stone Age, but it works while they're on a hunting expedition relatively close to the shore. Far out on the ocean, it is a totally different ballgame.

The speed at which Peary claims to have travelled is also impossible on the Arctic Ocean. Six miles (11 km) from the Pole, we left all our gear and proceeded on skis, carrying only light backpacks with windbreakers, cameras, and the GPS. Richard is a former member of the national cross-country ski team, yet we could do no better than two miles (4 km) per hour over average ice. This was verified by the GPS. Peary, who had lost most of his toes to frostbite, would have had a difficult time walking, so how, day after day, did he make two and a half to four miles (4.6 to 7.4 km) per hour, often leading the way?

Some people believe that Peary and Henson moved at a more constant, predictable rate, because they had dogs. That may be true in Greenland or along the cost, on a reasonably flat, smooth surface. But the ocean isn't the same thing at all. Because it's constantly changing, there is no such thing as a constant rate, dogs or no dogs. You can't travel in a straight line — you have to go around or across open water, up and down the pressure ridges. When we started back from the Pole, Will Steger and his dog teams were at least 160 miles (296 km), possibly 200 miles (370 km), ahead of us. When we reached Ward Hunt Island, he was still thirty miles (56 km) out on the ice. We travelled at least 50 per cent farther each day than the extremely experienced Steger and his dogs. A dog team can only work about ten hours, possibly twelve, per day on a regular basis; we kept going fourteen to twenty hours per day coming home from the Pole.

No expedition, supported or unsupported, no matter how experienced or inexperienced, benefitting from all that is now known about the Arctic, and with access to hi-tech equipment unimagined in Peary's day, has ever made the speeds Peary claimed to have made.

There is much else to puzzle over in Peary's accounts of his expeditions. Peary talks about wasting six days of good weather in March while waiting for a lead to freeze over so that he could cross it. Never, in all our experience, have we encountered a lead that we could not ski around in a few hours. And even on a relatively warm day in March, the mercury would still be around $-45°C$ ($-49°F$). At that temperature, water in a lead will freeze solid in a day.

It is accepted by many that Peary at least reached 87°47' north, because Bartlett, the expedition's ship captain, took his own independent reading at that latitude before turning back, leaving Peary and Henson to proceed on their own. But what is the proof that Peary was even that far north? There is only one sun shot attributed to Bartlett at 87°47. But one sun shot means nothing at that latitude without correcting or checking longitude so as to determine the exact moment of midday. Bartlett, however, was understandably satisfied after taking just one sun shot. It's unpleasant to lie there in the snow with a sextant and a bowl of mercury in $-45°C$ ($-49°F$) weather; anyone would want to keep the work to a minimum. As the entire party assumed they were not drifting, they assumed the local noon hadn't changed, hence no need to take more than one sun shot. But drifting they almost certainly were.

No one knows, and no one ever will know, where Peary really ended up.

APPENDIX E

THE FOLLOW US PROJECT
(report by David Adams)

The Follow Us project was the educational component of the 1995 Weber/Malakhov North Pole expedition. Students at Confederation High School (located in Nepean, Ontario, Canada), with the help of John Hindle and principal John Spence, hosted the project and became the focal point for approximately three hundred schools throughout the world. The project's primary objective was to capture the interest of students in science and the Arctic environment through the establishment of a direct satellite communication link with the two Arctic explorers, Richard Weber and Mikhail (Misha) Malakhov.

Two senior Confederation High School students, Tony Tam and David Adams, were asked to coordinate the project and gather a team of interested students from across all grades to act as an executive committee. This group, which included Julia Jozwiak, Shailla Nargundkar, Chris Mediratta, and Cara Filby, was to have full responsibility for the implementation and success of the project.

The communications system, known as TUBSAT (Technical University of Berlin Satellite), used a micro-satellite and a modified hand-held receiver that could store sixty-four characters at a time and transmit them to the satellite. Every hundred minutes, when the satellite passed over the Arctic Ocean, it could receive a message from Richard and Misha, which would then be downloaded when it passed over Confederation High School. (The satellite could also transmit messages to the explorers after receiving them from the students.) The students relayed Richard and Misha's messages via the Internet to schools in Russia, Romania, Italy, England, New Zealand, Australia, the United States, and Canada.

The participating students around the world followed the progress of Misha and Richard as they skied approximately 2,200 kilometres over a four-month period (from February to June 1995). Their schools were able to communicate with the expedition through the group of Confederation students who ran the computer centre.

The students had prepared about one hundred potential questions and had recorded responses from Richard and Misha before the two explorers left for the Pole. The information was supplemented by a team of science and geography students who conducted further research on the Arctic. When they were unable to come up with an answer, the students had the option of asking the trekkers questions through the satellite link, and Richard and Misha were usually able to respond the next day. Most questions were scientific, geographic, or personal. Information about the expedition was posted weekly on the Internet for the participating schools.

The Follow Us project received support from a number of organizations: Shaklee Canada, SchoolNet, Industry Canada, Natural Resources Canada, Northwest Power Corporation, Ottawa Carleton Research Institute, the Technical University of Berlin, and many others.

At the conclusion of the project in June 1995, several Confederation students met with eight Russian students who had also taken part in the project to exchange ideas and discuss their experiences. In addition, six students from Confederation and two Russian students flew to Resolute, N.W.T., to meet the explorers. One student from this group was selected to travel to Ward Hunt Island, the most northern point in Canada, for a special reunion.

Below, a couple of the students involved describe their experiences.

Tony Tam

(Tony was one of the project leaders. He is now studying Computer Engineering at Waterloo University.)

The Follow Us project was truly the very definition of a "once-in-a-lifetime" experience. On behalf of the students involved . . . I would like to thank Richard and Misha for providing this unique opportunity to follow history in the making. . . . One of the great things about the project was being charged with the responsibility of relaying information from Richard and Misha to the expedition manager and to the rest of the world. This gave us a tremendous sense of teamwork and we felt like an integral part of the expedition.

Our school sent out an invitation to schools around the world to follow the explorers along with us. As you might expect, applications came pouring in. The schools participating received a kit with slides, maps, etc. They also received regular updates and were given the option of asking us questions about the logistics of the trek, science, and the Arctic.

As a project leader, I was charged with designing a system to respond to the overwhelming amount of questions we expected to receive, getting interested students to participate, and eventually ensuring that the project ran smoothly. . . .

Not only was a system designed to handle questions, but a pen pal program, "Friends Around the World," was created. . . .

Students involved learned to use electronic mail and communicate with students around the world. We were also interviewed by the media and gave presentations to the trustees of the board of education, parents, and local schools. . . .

As with Richard and Misha, we experienced our own triumphs and disappointments. In the end, we had a great sense of pride in our work and knew that if we had an opportunity to do it again, we would have the experience to do it ten times better.

The project provided great enthusiasm to come to school. We were doing something that students . . . had not done before us. Like Richard and Misha, we were breaking new ground. . . .

Thank you Richard and Misha for the experience of a lifetime!!

Julia Jozwiak

(Julia was the TUBSAT communications expert on the project. She is now studying medicine at the University of Ottawa.)

As TUBSAT expert, I had a very big responsibility in keeping a continuous link of communication with both Richard and Misha. I was their only tie to the . . . world that they had left temporarily behind. . . . I looked forward to each day, anticipating Richard and Misha's next message. I didn't mind standing outside in the bitter cold of Canada's bone-chilling winter, waiting for the message to be transmitted from the satellite. I felt warmer knowing that Misha and Richard were experiencing much colder weather. By the end of the trek, I felt I had created a bond with Richard and Misha . . . simply through our daily satellite communications. It is as if I had been right there with them, experiencing their disappointments and accomplishments. . . .

I took part in presentations to parents and students who were . . . following the project through the Internet. Because this project was so technologically oriented, I managed to learn a little more about the future's computers, its programs, capabilities, and modes of communication. It was overwhelming to know that just by pressing a single button on the computer at school, I was relaying messages to the rest of the world!

It was a once-in-a-lifetime opportunity to have been one of the few people chosen to go up to Resolute and actually meet Richard and Misha . . . as they completed their odyssey. I also had the joy of meeting and forming new friendships with several Russian students who came to visit us in Canada to celebrate the project's success. It was a great honour and pleasure to have taken part in the making of history. . . . Richard and Misha's success . . . will continue to remind me that everything and anything is possible and within reach.

Shailla Nargundkar

(Shailla was responsible for coordinating the independent study projects undertaken by the students. She is completing her studies at J. S. Woodsworth Secondary School this year.)

When I volunteered for the Follow Us project, I never imagined the unforgettable experiences and excitement it would bring me. I became friends with many exceptional people during the project. Through these people, I have learned many things – from the mystery of the Arctic Ocean to the extraordinary culture of the Inuit people. I also gained a greater appreciation of my own country as I listened to the Russian students who came to Canada to take part in this wonderful experience with us. . . .

It was the raw excitement that kept our spirits high for those months. We had the utmost confidence in both Misha and Richard's capabilities. Through TUBSAT, we were able to trace their progress. We were their only link to civilization. News from both Canada and Russia was transmitted, as well as personal encouragement from their families. There was a lot of support and dedication filling the little room we had set aside for our project headquarters.

When I found out that I was one of the six students chosen for the trip to Resolute Bay, N.W.T., I was ecstatic – what an opportunity! We travelled there to congratulate Richard and Misha and celebrate their successful arrival in Resolute. We spent three days touring the small town of a few hundred people, and we were treated extremely well. My fellow adventurers and I found it quite amusing to come across a signpost showing the distance to different cities in the world, such as Tokyo (8,330 miles) and Moscow (6,331 miles). We visited local landmarks, such as an eight-hundred-year-old Inuit village and the local school. The trip was one of the most educational experiences in my life.

After a long wait and setbacks due to weather conditions, Misha and Richard arrived at the tiny airport in Resolute. They were exhausted, but managed to thank everyone for their participation in the Follow Us project. On our flight back to Ottawa, the plane was filled with laughter and excitement.

When we arrived back in Ottawa, there was a crowd waiting at the airport with welcome banners and Canadian flags. Everyone was waiting to get a glimpse of the explorers. Television news crews and newspaper reporters were ready with their cameras and notebooks to record the event. It was a great welcome home, and even the six of us got a little publicity. Misha and Richard made history trekking to the North Pole and back unassisted, and they deserved the attention that was waiting for them.

I am proud to have been a part of this historical event. Thank you.

APPENDIX F

INDEPENDENT CONFIRMATION OF
ARRIVAL AT THE POLE

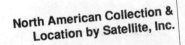

**North American Collection &
Location by Satellite, Inc.**

Worldwide Geo-Positioning and Data Collection

12 May 1995

Richard Weber
Weber Malakhov Expedition
513 Route 105
Box 106
Chelsea, Quebec GOX 1NO
CANADA

Dear Richard:

Congratulations to you and Misha!!!! We confirm your arrival at the pole. As I am sure you know, your Argos adventure beacon and the Argos data collection and location system is capable of calculating geo-positions anywhere on the Globe to within 150 meters. The following message was received by the Argos Processing Center in Landover, Maryland USA at 09:28:10 GMT today 12 May 1995:

```
00200   04005   5   5 J 1995-05-12   09:28:10   89.996   139.729  0.000   401649355
                1995-05-12   09:25:47  2  -.60541E+1                00          00
00
```

Your latitude of 89.996 is proof of your fantastic and courageous trek! I hope you and Misha receive this letter in good health and spirits. We at NACLS and the CLS family of companies again congratulate you and Misha and look forward to supporting any future endeavors you or Misha may undertake.

Sincerely,

Brian Hester
Project Engineer
Adventure Projects

APPENDIX G

1992 AND 1995 EXPEDITION SPONSORS

To all our sponsors, our sincerest thanks.

1992

Founding Sponsor
Alcatel Canada Wire

Major Sponsors
Kaufman Footwear Ltd.

Sustaining Sponsors
PRIO Bank of Ryazan, Russia
Malden Mills – Polartec Performance Challenge

Contributing Sponsors
First Air
Canada 125
Centre De La Diapo
Centre Pole
Chlorophylle Haut Technologie
Culture & Sport, External Affairs Canada
Kodak Canada
Makivik Corporation
Northern Stores
Technical University of Berlin

Supporting Sponsors
Aerographics
Above & Beyond Magazine
Alexander Battery Co.
A Newfoundland Bakery

Bollé Canada
Budapest Delicatessen
Canada Boy
Celestial Seasonings
Coleman
Dairy Bureau of Canada
Dupont Canada
Feathered Friends
Fischer Skis
Freeze-Dry Foods Limited
Gatineau Park
Igloo Vikski
André Moreau
Nalge Company
Norca Industries
Ostrom Outdoors
Paris Gloves of Canada
Shaklee Canada
Sportsmart
Sporteque de Hull
Swix Ski Poles
Thorlo Socks
Trailhead
Westin Foods
Zippy Print

1995

Patron Sponsor
Kaufman Footwear Ltd.

Major Sponsors
First Air
Michel Perron

Sustaining Sponsors
Aeroflot

PRIO Bank of Ryazan, Russia
Malden Mills – Polartec Performance Challenge
Shaklee Canada

Contributing Sponsors
Centre De La Diapo
Centre Pole
Peter Green
Tim Kenny
Gérard Lebeau
Malden Mills – Polartec Performance Challenge
Navarro
Northern Stores
Jean & Richard Perron
Rolex Watch Company
Technical University of Berlin
Sony of Canada Limited

Supporting Sponsors
Above & Beyond Magazine
Alexander Battery Co.
Atelier Gérard Eber
Bollé Canada
Budapest Delicatessen
Canada Boy
Canadian Centre for Marine Communication
Celestial Seasonings
Coleman
Crown Cap (1987) Ltd.
Cullity Restorations
Dupont Canada
Duracell
Eveready
Fischer Skis
Freeze-Dry Foods Limited
Garmin GPS
Tim Goodsell

Hewlett Packard
Igloo Vikski
Jeff Mantell
McCain Refrigerated Foods
André Moreau
Narwhal Hotel, Resolute Bay
Ostrom Outdoors
Ottawa Carleton Research Institute
Paris Gloves of Canada
RAB Down Equipment
Rocky Mountain Chocolates
Performance Printing
Pierre Simard
SpaceQuest
Sportsmart
Surrey Satellite Technology Laboratory
Systems Engineering Society
Swix Ski Poles
Terramar/Resolute
Thiokol Co.
Alan Thompson & Co.
Thorlo Socks
Telemedicine Centre, Memorial University of Newfoundland
Texcan
Traveling Light
Winnipeg Fur Exchange
Zippy Print

ACKNOWLEDGEMENTS

For both our 1992 and 1995 expeditions, there were so many people who helped along the way. We were just two on the ice, but backing us up each time was a host of people without whom there would never have been an expedition.

Kaufman Footwear Ltd. supported us from the very beginning, with vice-president Jack Thomas believing in us when the Pole was just a dream. He was assisted by Bob Rutter, Tony Dowling, and John Barnes. Jim Chadwick designed us the best winter boots in the world.

Peter Green was the first person to back his belief in our project with a financial contribution, corporately in 1992, as president of Alcatel Canada Wire, and personally in 1995.

Our volunteer radio operators, Jean Castonguay and Vasiliy Zaushitsyn, spent hundreds of hours listening for our calls. Liane Benoit worked tirelessly for many months in 1991 and 1992.

In 1992, Gilles Couet at Chlorophylle Haut Technology helped design and make our clothing.

The 1995 expedition would never have happened without the support of Michel and Lise Perron and their North Pole Light companions, Tim Kenny, Gerard Lebeau, Jeff Mantell, Jean Perron, and Pierre Simard.

John Spence, principal of Confederation High School, and administrator John Hindle, had the vision to organize the Follow Us project. Our communications for the project were handled by David Adams, Tony Tam, Julia Jozwiak, Chris Mediratta, Shailla Nargundkar, and Cara Filby. In Germany, Professor Udo Renner kept the satellite in orbit. Ekhard Krabel trained us to use TUBSAT.

While we were training in Iqaluit, the people were wonderfully friendly and helpful, often stopping us on the street to wish us good luck. In particular, we would like to thank Larry Horlick, who helped us with all our electronic gear, including training us on the Televilt beacon. When our polar clothing arrived but did not fit, Jane Cooper re-tailored it. Mikhim Construction and Bronyk Skavinsky housed us in their employee bunkhouses. Fred Coman let us store our equipment in his warehouse. Ken MacRury was a wealth of information on the North and found us the seal-hook which was so critical, not only for landing a seal, but also for getting across leads. Our old friends and trail companions, Brent Boddy and Donny Coglan, were often around to give a helping hand. Andy Terriault lent us his workshop to prepare skis and sleds. The bear scares for the depot were armed with black powder by Dick Smith. Our visitors Tim Goodsell, Kent Humphrey, and Mark Fuller helped pack our gear. Nobu Norita and Atsushi Miyagawa kept us company training.

We owe a special word of thanks to First Air and all its employees. We know that we were always flown in the greatest safety possible, and First Air personnel helped us far beyond what would normally be expected of an airline company. In particular, our thanks to Andy Campbell, Rudy Kellar, Greg White, Fred Alt, and especially Pat "Bomber" Doyle, who landed us at Ward Hunt Island in the pitch dark.

Lena Kashina took our diaries and created a text in Russian. Ed Hailwood moulded hundreds of pages of "Russian" English into a book. At McClelland & Stewart, Alex Schultz put everything together and kept the project moving forward.

Thanks to Meg and Hans Weber, who revealed the Arctic to their son.

More than anything, we are grateful to our wives, Josée and Olga. They had the courage to be there always — helping, supporting, believing — not just through these two expeditions, but through years of polar travel.